# Coping With Two Cultures

# Multilingual Matters

Alsatian Acts of Identity
    LILIANE M. VASSBERG
Attitudes and Language
    COLIN BAKER
Breaking the Boundaries
    EUAN REID and HANS H. REICH (eds)
Called unto Liberty
    COLIN H. WILLIAMS
Citizens of This Country: The Asian British
    MARY STOPES-ROE and RAYMOND COCHRANE
Continuing to Think: The British Asian Girl
    BARRIE WADE and PAMELA SOUTER
Education of Chinese Children in Britain and the USA
    LORNITA YUEN-FAN WONG
Equality Matters
    H. CLAIRE, J. MAYBIN and J. SWANN (eds)
European Models of Bilingual Education
    HUGO BAETENS BEARDSMORE (ed.)
Immigrant Languages in Europe
    GUUS EXTRA and LUDO VERHOEVEN (eds)
Multilingualism and Nation Building
    GERDA MANSOUR
One Europe - 100 Nations
    ROY N. PEDERSEN
Opportunity and Constraints of Community Language Teaching
    SJAAK KROON
The World in a Classroom
    V. EDWARDS and A. REDFERN

**Please contact us for the latest book information:**
**Multilingual Matters Ltd, Frankfurt Lodge, Clevedon Hall,**
**Victoria Road, Clevedon, Avon BS21 7SJ, England**

**MULTILINGUAL MATTERS 99**
Series Editor: Derrick Sharp

# Coping With Two Cultures

## British Asian and Indo-Canadian Adolescents

Paul A. Singh Ghuman

**MULTILINGUAL MATTERS LTD**
Clevedon • Philadelphia • Adelaide

**Library of Congress Cataloging in Publication Data**

Ghuman, Paul A. Singh (Paul Avtar Singh), 1936-
Coping With Two Cultures: British Asian and Indo-Canadian Adolescents/
Paul A. Singh Ghuman.
p. cm. (Multilingual Matters: 99)
Includes bibliographical references and index
1. Asian students–England–Birmingham–Attitudes. 2. Asian students–British
Columbia–Vancouver–Attitudes. 3. Asian students–England–Birmingham–.
Social conditions. 4. Asian students–British Columbia–Vancouver–
Social conditions. 5. Ethnicity–England–Birmingham. 6. Ethnicity–British
Columbia–Vancouver. I. Title. II. Title: Coping With Two Cultures. III. Series:
Multilingual Matters (Series): 99.
LC3736.G62B574    1993
371.97'95'041–dc20

**British Library Cataloguing in Publication Data**

A CIP catalogue record for this book is available from the British Library.

ISBN 1-85359-202-1 (hbk)
ISBN 1-85359-201-3 (pbk)

**Multilingual Matters Ltd**

*UK*: Frankfurt Lodge, Clevedon Hall, Victoria Road, Clevedon, Avon BS21 7SJ.
*USA*: 1900 Frost Road, Suite 101, Bristol, PA 19007, USA.
*Australia*: P.O. Box 6025, 83 Gilles Street, Adelaide, SA 5000, Australia.

Cover design by Bob Jones Associates.
Typeset by Editorial Enterprises.
Printed and bound in Great Britain by the Longdunn Press, Bristol.

This book is dedicated to the memory of my sister, Mohinder, and my nephew, Jimmy

# Contents

# List of Tables

# Preface

It has become almost a part of folk wisdom in Britain and North America to claim that second-generation Asian young people suffer from a so-called identity crisis. Are they Indian, English, British-Muslims or Asians? Discussion on this and related issues has been based mainly on reports in the popular press and TV (often of isolated cases), e.g. media coverage of distress cases of Asian girls leaving home or rebelling against arranged marriages. There is a paucity of comprehensive and in-depth information in this area of social and educational concern. This is particularly worrying when applied to the training of students wishing to become teachers, social workers or school counsellors in a multicultural society.

This volume makes a contribution to this end. It is based on two research projects carried out in England and Canada. The English studies were undertaken in Birmingham, where a large sample (463) of Asian students of Hindu, Sikh and Muslim extraction completed a questionnaire and an acculturation scale. Additionally, a sample of 50 young people from the larger sample were interviewed to probe further into their opinions and attitudes towards life in multicultural British society. To this end, they were asked questions regarding their family life, choice of friends and clothes, favourite school subjects, equality of boys and girls and personal identity.

To obtain a more comprehensive picture on the above-mentioned topics, a small group of parents (24), teachers (27), social workers (2) and community leaders (4) were interviewed in informal settings.

In order to provide a cross-cultural perspective on these controversial issues and on the anxieties of young people (age 13 to 16), cognate samples of students, parents, teachers and community leaders were studied in Vancouver, Canada. Similar research techniques to the one used in Birmingham were employed in Vancouver to collect information. All this data was further enriched by informal conversations and observation, both in Birmingham and Vancouver. I have also maintained continuing professional contacts with schools in Birmingham where the studies were conducted, both as a teacher and as a teacher trainer. All these experiences have been woven into the text where relevant.

Chapter 1 offers a general background account of immigrants from the Indian sub-continent along with their main cultural and religious beliefs and practices. Also, in this Chapter the problems and concerns of the second-generation are identified and the methods of investigation are discussed. Chapter 2 is fundamental. In it, detailed analyses and discussion of the questionnaire and attitude scale used are presented. In addition, there is a lengthy examination and presentation of interview data and a brief discussion of previous studies.

Chapters 3, 4 and 5 contain detailed discussions of the responses of teachers, parents and community leaders respectively. All three Chapters are based on the data collected through semi-structured interviews. In the final Chapter, an attempt is made to synthesise the findings of the current investigations and to highlight the ensuing (emerging) issues.

The technical aspects of the data are kept to the minimum to enhance the readability of the text for those unfamiliar with research techniques. Extracts from the interviews have been liberally used to offer a flavour of the sensibilities involved. The majority of parents and community leaders preferred to use their home languages during the interviews — in most cases Punjabi, Urdu or Hindi. I have myself translated the relevant extracts into English for inclusion in the text. The choice of these was essentially subjective, but I was guided by the wish to provide as comprehensive a picture as I could of the relevant issues and to ensure that the intensity of feeling of those involved would be fully demonstrated.

At the outset, I feel it is important to state my own views on multiculturism. I am personally committed to the ideals which underpin cultural diversity, namely those of tolerance, understanding and the fascination of being 'human' in so many different ways. To what extent this outlook colours my perceptions and interpretations, I leave to the reader to judge.

# Acknowledgements

This work would not have been possible without the generous help and support of many people and organisations. I am very grateful to all the students, parents, teachers, counsellors, headmasters and community leaders who so freely gave of their time. I owe a debt of gratitude to my friends (Harminder, Brian, Paul, Maria and Santokh) and relatives at Nottingham who helped me through very many informal discussion, chats and enquiries.

I heartly appreciate the active and ready support of my colleagues at the University of Wales, Aberystwyth: in particular, I would like to mention Professor Gareth Elwyn Jones, Bob Morris Jones, Rick Lloyd, Daniel Chandler and Geoff Evans. For typing I am grateful to Shân Hayward, Meinir Jenkins, Sheila Duggan and Geoff Evans.

I acknowledge with deep appreciation the financial support from the following: The Vice-Principal's Fund, the Welsh-Canadian Association and the Faculty of Education, University of Wales.

I am indebted to the Vancouver School Board for allowing me to research in two schools under their jurisdiction.

In spite of such willing support, all errors or omissions are entirely my own.

# Glossary of Asian Words

**Bat:** To speak English
**Biraderi/Bhai-Chara:** Extended family net-work
**Bhai:** Sikh priest also brother
**Brahmin:** Hindu priest
**Chappati:** Home-made Indian/Pakistani bread
**Chamar:** Harijan, a low caste person
**Durga:** Hindu goddess of 'skhati' (power)
**Gora:** White people
**Gurudwara:** Sikh temple
**Gurumukhi:** Written script for Punjabi
**Izzat:** Honour
**Jat:** Farmer
**Kameez:** Long-sleeves woman's shirt
**Kali:** Hindu goddess of destruction
**Mandir:** Hindu temple
**Masjid:** Mosque
**Nai:** Barber
**Guru Nanak:** The founder of Sikh religion
**Paratha:** Butter cooked Indian/Pakistani bread
**Parvati:** Consort of Shiva
**Pukka house:** Brick built house
**Rupee:** Indian and Pakistani currency
**Sarsawati:** Hindu Goddess of knowledge and wisdom
**Salwar:** Baggy Indian/Pakistani style trousers
**Shiva:** Hindu God of destruction

# 1 Setting the Scene

> I contacted a dalal and paid £300 deposit for my brother's immigration. Altogether it cost me £600 but it was worth it. He joined me in 1962. Then I managed to have four more relatives join me here in Birmingham.... They have done well.

Migration has always been and probably will remain a feature of human society. People have always migrated from region to region, state to state and country to country — to seek opportunities to improve their economic and cultural level or to escape from persecution. In the post-colonial period (1947 onwards) the size and scope of migration increased to unprecedented levels. Thus, for example, those who have come into Britain include workers from the Caribbean, Asia, Africa, Eire and the old Commonwealth countries. Obviously there was a great need for unskilled labour in all the industrialised European countries in the 1950s and 1960s where immigrants are thought to be beneficial to the economy (otherwise they would never have been encouraged to come in the first place), though problems of community relations have arisen.Our concern in this book is with the immigrants from the Asian sub-continent. The main aim of this chapter is to provide the reader with background information on the South Asians (East Indians as they are termed in Canada), so that the concerns and anxieties of the youngsters can be fully appreciated and understood in their historical and social contexts.

The approach here is different from other available works (Desai, 1963; Ballard & Ballard, 1979; Anwar, 1979; Shaw, 1988; Ghuman, 1975) in that the participants describe their own first-hand experiences of immigration, settlement, value systems and the like rather than lengthy factual and tabular accounts. To this end I interviewed a number of first-generation parents in Birmingham and Vancouver. I did my field work in Vancouver in 1990, where I interviewed 20 Indo-Canadians belonging to Hindu and Sikh religions. In Birmingham field work was carried out a year earlier, where seven Sikhs (five males and two females), seven Hindus (four males and three females) and ten Muslims (all males) were interviewed. A tape-recorder was used throughout the field work. All parents preferred to be interviewed in their home language which was either Punjabi, Urdu or Hindu. Details of interviewing techniques, their reliability and value are discussed later on in the chapter.

Before the Second World War the total population of Asians living in Britain (Kondapi, 1949) was around 5,000: this included 1,000 general medical practitioners and 1,000 or so other professionals and students; the rest were mainly seamen (in Cardiff, Bristol and Liverpool) and tradesmen (mostly Sikh pedlars who found their way to the United Kingdom after a period of service in the armed forces). In 1939 there were only 100 Asians in Birmingham including 20 doctors plus students and teachers. Even in 1953 the estimate for the Indo-Pakistani population was only 2,000.

A Sikh pedlar from Birmingham of early settlement (1949) related his experiences.

> We were only three Sikhs in Cardiff — came after the second war and stayed on. Our trade was in clothes. We used to buy from the wholesalers and take it to the countryside. Life was hard we used to get homesick, but it was so expensive to go back. We saved money for our families and lived on very little. We shared a house with other Indians. There was communal cooking and sharing of other facilities.At that time there were so few Indians — we had problems buying our food. We knew a little 'bat' (English) to do business, but mostly we lived within the house and never ventured to go out. We wanted to save as much as we could to return home.

Likewise in Canada there were only a few thousand persons of South Asian origin before the onset of the 1950s. For instance in Vancouver there were only 555 labourers and 335 small business men in 1951. Here is an account given by a Sikh (one of the early settlers) in 'The Longest Journey' (Buchignani *et al.*, 1985: 14).

> My brother Kapur Singh was one of the first Sikhs to go to Canada. He soon wrote back to our village saying that work was available at Rs. 7a day — a princely sum in those days. Sixteen of us assembled to go off and try our luck. I was just eighteen. Some were reserve army men, but most were farmer's sons. After a quick train trip to Calcutta and a short voyage to Hong Kong we had to wait quite a while for the next ship to Canada. We were on the '113 boat' that arrived in Vancouver in October 1906. We were very worried about being rejected because of disease or some other reason — I think I aged two years — but not one of us was. (Tara Singh Sidoo).

A vivid account of the day-to-day life and tribulations of the early settlers in Vancouver is given by Dhami in his interesting and gripping book called 'Maluka' (Dhami, 1988).

Immigration to the United Kingdom increased dramatically after the Second World War. The 1948 Nationality Act gave Commonwealth citizens the right to enter the United Kingdom without visas or work permits. The causes of immigration of people from one country to another are manifold, but scholars such as Watson (1979) and Anwar (1979) tend to explain them under the categories of 'pull and push factors'. The major push factors may include massive upheavals of population through war, persecution and famine/or acute scarcity. The major pull factor is the commonsensical one of the improvement of the family's financial and social position. The other pull factor is the active encouragement given by the receiving society to the citizens of other countries through the prospect of better jobs, housing and recreational facilities. British emigration to Australia, Canada and New Zealand till the mid-1960s highlights this phenomenon. Likewise there was active recruitment of Afro-Caribbeans from the West Indies by the London Transport and Catering Association (Rose *et al.*, 1969).

India was partitioned in 1947 to create a homeland for the Muslims. There was large-scale migration of Hindus and Sikhs from the newly created Pakistan to India and of Muslims in the opposite direction. Nearly four million people were displaced in this upheaval. The most affected states were the Punjab, Bengal, Jammu and Kashmir.

Here we have a comment on this situation from a Sikh settled in Birmingham (factory worker).

> As soon as we heard we (Sikhs and Hindus) are going to be in a minority in Pakistan we knew we had to leave. But how? We were being attacked by our Muslim neighbours and village folk. There was arson, looting and senseless massacres. Our izzat (honour) was at stake; Muslims are known to abduct Sikh and Hindu girls throughout 400 years of Muslim invasions of India. Those were terrible times.

A Muslim shopkeeper commented on the situation:

> We had a good farm in Kamalpur — small but productive. It was all a Muslim village, very close knit. Then we heard stories of attacks on our communities by Sikhs. There was senseless butchery in so called 'revenge attacks' for the Sikhs killed in Pakistan. We had to leave, but how? That year (1947) there were heavy rains and the flooded river Sutlej caused havoc, thousands were drowned in the floods.

This upheaval in the sub-continent, especially in the Punjab, provided a stimulus for a significant number to seek their fortunes abroad, particularly in the United Kingdom, Canada and America. There has been a tradition of both internal and external migration in the Punjab which goes back to the early years of this century. A large number of small farmers (240,000) left the overcrowded East Punjab districts of Jallundur and Hoshiarpur for the West Punjab during the period 1921 to 1931, when the new canal system opened up vast areas of agricultural land

(Aurora, 1967). Then there was also seasonal migration to these newly opened areas to help with the cotton and wheat harvests. As regards emigration abroad, ex-soldiers and craftsmen sought their fortune in Hong Kong, British-held parts of Africa and as far as Australia (Ballard & Ballard, 1979).

A Sikh teacher commented:

We had nothing left when we came to Jullundur from Pakistan — just the clothes we were wearing. We were in a refugee camp for six months.Then we were allotted 10 acres of land per household. A small grant was also given for buying some agricultural implements. It was a miserable existence. I then vowed to emigrate abroad, preferably to Canada because I could farm there or work on a farm.

There was another upheaval in the Mirpur district of Kashmir in 1962. About 100,000 people were displaced because the government planned to build a dam to generate electricity and store water for agriculture.

Displaced persons were given adequate compensation to start life afresh. Similarly the other two main areas of emigration, Mirpur and Campbellpur in Pakistan and the Sylhet district in Bangladesh, have a history of travelling abroad. The British shipping companies used to recruit seamen from these areas to obtain a cheap and reliable work force (Ballard & Ballard, 1979). Here we have a verbatim report from a Mirpuri Muslim:

We lost everything our houses, land and friends. I felt desperate. Being head of the family — as my father died a few years ago — I had to plan for the family. We bought a small house in the Punjab but there wasn't much to do. Then I heard people are going to England for 5,000 rupees. I approached this 'dalal' (agent) who got my passport in six months and I was in Bradford with a friend soon after.

The second push factor relates to the scarcity of farming land in the Punjab and other states on the Indian sub-continent. For instance in the Jallundur district of the Punjab 25% of land holdings are less than one acre (Rose *et al.*, 1969: 52). A Sikh belonging to Jallundur district comments:

We're five brothers — had only three acres of land between us. My three brothers were married with kids. We had two sisters of marriageable age — for whom we had to find dowries. There was just not enough money to go around. Then my father contacted a dalal (agent) and he demanded 5,000 rupees. My father raised the money by mortgaging an acre of our farm. My passage was arranged and I was in Birmingham with a relative. I have sent money regularly and also sponsored my two brothers to come to England. Though I have had hard times I don't regret it.

It is important to emphasise that poverty is not the reason why a large number of people from Punjab, Sylhet and Mirpur have migrated. The migrants were the middle classes of their country of origin. It took a lot of initiative, resources and drive to raise finances (sometimes well over £500 in the 1960s) and venture abroad with no English and no technical skills.

Furthermore migration abroad invariably brought prosperity in visible terms, a 'pukka house' (brick built) was a big status symbol. The family's izzat (honour) was raised through migration (Jai Singh Englandia — Jai Singh from England or Bhag Canadia), and the next generation could expect better education and marriage proposals for the young from well-off and high status families. To illustrate another pull factor we have a comment from a Hindu respondent (electrician):

> In a way I had a reasonable job in a factory. I was a skilled welder. I was getting quite good pay but could not save much for my children's education and marriages. This village friend of mine ended up in Toronto — he used to send loads of money to his family. They could afford a radio and other luxury goods. They always offered us tea and sweets (made of pure white sugar! — it was considered as a status symbol) to guests. I thought I should take the plunge. Now I have been in Birmingham for 30 years — I don't regret it. I have my own house, kids are in colleges and I have a secure future in Britain.

## Chain Migration

As the name suggests chain migration takes place through an established network of family members, kinsmen, relatives and sometimes through friends. For instance, the eldest son from a family came to England and established himself and then arranged for his brother's passage, who in turn sponsored his wife's brother and so on. Here we have a vivid account of this process from a Hindu graduate, now a bus driver.

> I came to England in 1959. Got a job as a bus conductor, I worked overtime and made £30 a week on average — a lot of money at that time. I spent £5 on food and rent and saved the rest. Some I sent home and the rest went on a house deposit; I could rent out rooms then. I contacted a dalal and paid £300 deposit for my brother's immigration. Altogether it cost me £600 but it was worth it. He joined me in 1962. Then I managed to have four more relatives join me here in Birmingham. I also helped them to get jobs in foundries. They all have done well.

Chain migration was the principal mode of entry to Canada until 1969. To take an extreme example, chain migration has guaranteed that many of 9,000 Fijian Indians or the 30,000 Sikhs in the Vancouver area are related to each other (Buchignani *et al*, 1985: 173).

Here we have an extract from Khan's research on the Mirpuris to illustrate the pull of England leading to chain migration (Khan, 1979: 89) which confirms our findings.

> However much they save in Britain by village standards they return rich, well dressed and with a knowledge of the outside world. Symbols of success (e.g. clothes, watches and suitcases) and reports of the new life create a half-picture, a distorted image. The difficulties encountered in 'Villayat' and still to be faced on return are minimised to ensure the delight and pride of family and kin.

Here we have the story of a Muslim, Muhammad Ali, given by Green in his book 'Them' (Green, 1990: 29).

> My father had come here in 1956, one of the first Pakistanis to come. He came to improve his standard of living, to earn some money and go back home. He came to live here at most for five years. Make some money, go back home, buy some land or some property and just earn enough to live by so that he could give his children a good start in life. But he never did go back. It is in human nature that whatever you've made, you always want to make more. Like gambling 'let's stay for another year and make some more and then with more money when we go back we'll be able to buy more land'. But the longer they stayed the more they became involved with the social life of this country. Then they brought over their families and that was really the turning point.

Immigration from the Indian sub-continent to the United Kingdom peaked in 1961 because of the anxieties generated by the news that the government was about to bring in a bill to restrict the entry of peoples from India and Pakistan.

> The sudden change in migration movements in 1961 when net flow increased six-fold over the previous year is explicable in terms of three factors affecting immigration. First there was the fear of control in Britain. This affected the organisation of transport and the activities of travel agents in India and Pakistan who exploited and helped to create the demand ... the effect of the Commonwealth Immigration Act was not only to increase the number of immigrants in this country but also to increase the rate of arrivals to such an extent that in eighteen months the net inflow was almost as great as that of the previous five years (Rose *et al.*, 1969: 77).

Few migrants came with the intention of settling down in the United Kingdom. Most thought that they would work really hard for a few years, live frugally, save a lot of money and finally return to their kith and kin. However, with the passage of time they were getting used to good wages (they always multiplied the £1 by 20 to express their wages in rupees for comparison), the provisions of the welfare state and particularly the high value which they placed on English education. This was often cryptically summed up in the phrase 'Villayat is like a sweet prison'. The real crisis came with the threat to stop all forms of immigration into the United Kingdom in 1960–61 (Fryer, 1984). In some way the decision was made for them; most migrants, Sikhs in particular, started sending for their families before the Bill came into operation.

The first immigration act was passed in 1962 and took away from all Commonwealth citizens the automatic right to enter the United Kingdom except for those issued with vouchers. However, wives and children under sixteen were free to accompany or join husbands or parents already here (Rose *et al.*, 1969: 87). Immigration from the Indian sub-continent after 1962 became highly selective; teachers, doctors, engineers and scientists were issued vouchers in increasingly large numbers. For instance, a total of 1,113 vouchers were issued to people with special skills in the period 1965–67. Three types of vouchers were introduced by the 1962 Act:

A    for those with specific jobs to come to;

B    for those who possessed special skills; and

C    for unskilled workers.

The C-type voucher was discontinued in August 1965 (the Ministry stopped issuing them in August 1964).

Here we have a comment from a lecturer:

I was deputy head of a 13+ school in the Punjab in 1967. I was close to my village and pay was good. I was due for promotion to headship but I had high hopes of travel and further education in England. I applied for a B voucher. I got it straight away. At that time teachers and doctors were given vouchers without delay. I arrived in Nottingham soon after.

Primary immigration to the United Kingdom virtually ceased with the passing of the 1971 Immigration Act. This Act restricted the entry of dependants and allowed new entrants only to take up specific jobs for a limited period of time, e.g., the management committee of a Gurudwara could apply for a 'Bhai' (priest) on the grounds that trained priests are not available in the United Kingdom (Fryer, 1984).

## South Asians From East Africa

It is important to mention, albeit briefly, another group of South Asians who emigrated to Britain between the mid-1960s and early 1970s from East Africa mostly from Uganda, Kenya and Malawi. They are the descendants of indentured labourers hired in 1896 to build railways in Uganda by the Imperial British East Africa Company. Most of them retained their British passports after the independence of the above countries. They wanted to keep open their option of settling in the United Kingdom should political or social difficulties arise.

Soon after independence policies of Africanisation were adopted by the three countries resulting in the uprooting of the Asian community. President Idi Amin's policies went beyond the opening of jobs for the indigenous blacks and became life threatening for the Asians. Increasingly, large numbers of Asians began to emigrate to the United Kingdom in the mid-1960s (Bhachu, 1988a).

To stop this influx of Asians from East Africa an emergency bill was passed in the United Kingdom parliament in 1968. The Act withdrew the automatic right of entry given to British subjects under the 1948 Nationality Act and introduced a new clause granting entry rights to British passport holders only if they could prove patrial connections, i.e. that parents or grandparents were born in the United Kingdom.

According to Rex & Tomlinson (1979: 50) 'clearly the Act of 1968 went a long way in distinguishing *de facto* 'between white and coloured citizens'. A separate quota for immigration was established for East African Asians to enter the United Kingdom and the Canadian and Australian governments were also persuaded to take small numbers of uprooted Asians. A vivid account from Green's book Them (Green, 1990: 65–6) illustrates this. Ramesh Vala says:

> After primary education (in Kenya) I went to secondary school, the Duke of Gloucester School. This was an Asian equivalent of a British public school. I wanted to be a lawyer, I'd wanted to be a lawyer when I was eight. I can't explain it. We had an English teacher from Warwickshire and he told me that if I wanted to do law there was only one place: the London School of Economics. I was brash enough to think I would get in, and luckily, I did. In 1963 the idea was that if you were British and if you held on to your passport you had the right to come to Britain. That stopped in 1968 after which you had to apply for a visa, to get a voucher, rather than just come. In 1968 those who reckoned there would be a better life in Britain came over; the very rich had already moved most of their money out, but they didn't want to leave, they had a terrific life in Kenya. It wasn't as dramatic an exodus as what happened in Uganda. This was a matter of 3,000 people rushing out in a week because of what the Labour government in

London was doing on immigration. In Uganda you had 30,000 who were driven out by Amin. But there were all these people working out the best way to get into England: if you came via Dublin you weren't stopped — they assumed you were coming from Europe — whereas if you came in direct you were likely to be stopped, you were likely to spend some time in a detention centre.

The East African Asians were somewhat different from the direct immigrants on a number of counts: they had a good command of English, urban skills and capital to facilitate their adjustment to the United Kingdom. Although they wanted to emphasise their separateness from the direct immigrants from the sub-continent this perceived exclusiveness was only valid within Asian communities. The whites regarded all of 'them' as Hindus, 'Pakis' or Sikhs.

## Migration to British Columbia

The Canadian immigration laws prior to 1967 were extremely discriminatory against the South Asians and people from other Third World countries. As a consequence the immigration from India and Pakistan was negligible; for example the 1952 Immigration Act set a low quota of 450 people from the whole Indian sub-continent (Bhatnagar, 1981).

Sikhs were the first settlers in and around Vancouver in the years 1903–1906. However, their total population in British Columbia was not greater than 4,000 in 1961. After 1961 there was a steady in-flow of educated professionals from urban backgrounds to British Columbia. The 1967 Immigration Act laid out non-racial criteria for entry into Canada: as a result there was a sharp rise in the number of immigrants with professional backgrounds. The arrival pattern is summarised in Table 1.1.

Here is the story of a Hindu Canadian immigrant who has been in Vancouver for 20 years:

All my friends went abroad, I was the only one left in Nawashahar (Punjab). I used to get nice letters from Vancouver — how wonderful things are. There were only two ways of going as I am not a professional — through marriage or as a visitor and then stay on. My mother tried our relatives who had kith and kin abroad and finally she found a suitable match. The girl was in the Punjab but had her Canadian papers because of her father. I got married but it took eighteen months before I could come. I have worked in a saw-mill, cannery and as a taxi driver. All these jobs are very hard but it's OK now I am settled here.

A Sikh relates his experience as follows.

I came to Canada in 1957 as a young boy of thirteen. I went to school but did not learn very much. I left school at fifteen and went to work in the nearby saw-mill. I worked there for twenty-five years ending up as a foreman. I had an arranged marriage and two kids. With my savings I have bought this strawberry farm. Here I have a big house now, kids at university and my wife is working in a real estate business. Things are very good now.

**Table 1.1** South Asians in British Columbia

| Year | Total |
|------|-------|
| 1903–1906 | 100 |
| 1921 | 951 |
| 1940 | 2000 |
| 1951 | 2148 |
| 1961 | 4526 |
| 1971 | 18995 |

Source: Buchignani *et al.* (1985).

## Settlement Patterns

Chain immigration ensured that newcomers would settle along family, caste, village and religious lines. Here we have the report of a Sikh teacher:

I came to my relative in Handsworth near Soho Road in 1959. To start with I shared a room with him. Later I got my own room but on the same road. He got me a job in a foundry in Smethwick. Handsworth was becoming very much like a Punjabi town at home.

A Muslim factory worker comments:

My distant relative was in Balsall Heath — so naturally I went there to stay with him. He helped me a lot. I got a job in a factory — it was hard shift work and very dirty but I persevered.

The new-comers settled mostly in the inner-city areas of British cities and Birmingham was no exception. There are Muslims in Small Heath, Balsall Heath and Lady Pool and Sikhs and Hindus in Handsworth and Edgbaston.

In these areas network ties of 'Bhai-Chara'/'Biraderi' have been recreated by the communities. These ties have provided security, continuity and stability to the communities.

Bath (1972) carried out an analysis of the spatial patterns of settlement of Punjabis from India and found that the house ownership pattern recreated closely the Punjabi village scene. Adjacent houses were bought on Bhai-Chara (Kith and Kin), religious and caste bases. Even the patronage of local public houses was along the lines of caste, religion, village and Bhai-Chara.

Shaw's (1988) study of a Pakistani community in Oxford shows that the early settlement in east Oxford was based on village and kinship networks.

There were a number of houses on St Clements, James and Circus streets in east Oxford occupied mainly by Jhelumi migrants whilst houses in other east Oxford streets including several on Bullingdon Road contained mainly people from Gujar Khan, Rawlpindi and Attock (Shaw, 1988: 41).

## Life Styles and Jobs

Most immigrants until the early 1960s were male, young to middle aged, and lived in all male households. They saved as much as they could to send money home and to pay for the passages of other relatives. A comment from a Hindu bus conductor illustrates this situation:

When I arrived in Birmingham in 1958 I had to share a room with another person. Rates were ten shillings (50p) for a shared bed (i.e. on shift work basis), one pound for a shared room usually with three to four people and £2 for a room. Then we have to pay for our communal 'langar' (cooking) and take turns to make chappatis and cook vegetable and lentil curries. I could save fifteen pounds a week. It was a lot of money at that time. My other experience was a few pints of beer over weekends. Life was routine and dull. I did as much overtime as I could get. There was only 'lino' on the floor and very occasionally 'Gymna' (landlord) would light a coal fire in the dining room. So it was always cold in the house. For our baths we had to go to the public baths near Handsworth park. It used to be freezing cold in winter. We listened to Punjabi folk music and Hindi pop a lot. There was camaraderie in the house; we talked a lot about the Punjab and how we missed it.

Teachers and other professionals who came on the 'voucher system' during the period 1962–65 found it hard to obtain professional jobs. A Sikh teacher laments:

> I was a College Lecturer in the Punjab with a higher degree and a law degree. My qualifications were approved by the DES. I applied to the Birmingham LEA for a teaching post. I was interviewed but turned down, maybe because I wore a turban, or my English was not good enough, or plain racism. So I got a job in the Post Office as a postman. That was in 1963. I applied to several authorities but no success. Eventually I got a teaching job in Birmingham in 1975.

It was not always easy to find a job even for unskilled persons. The lucky ones had relatives and friends who fixed everything for them. There were others who took a chance. Here is an account by a Hindu who is a skilled machinist who came to England in 1964 as reported by Sharma:

> He was a son of my village. But he was most unwilling to put me up so I said to him 'I have only three pounds and no job'. I know now that I made a great mistake in leaving a job where I earned plenty and had a house which only cost me four rupees a month. I was not badly off. but now I have made this mistake and it is too late to go back (Sharma, 1971: 79).

Here we have an extract from Anwar's book 'The Myth of Return' (Anwar, 1979: 186) which reports similar experiences of Muslims.

> On arrival in Rochdale they stayed with relatives and the one who was still without family here continued to do so. Once settled they each sponsored other relatives and aided them by getting work vouchers … due to the nature of their work they slept almost all day. All activities outside work took place among immediate relatives and the Biraderi (kinsfolk) They regarded Western education and their non-Muslim surroundings as a threat to their religion and their values.

## Family Life

After the initial period of staying in all male houses, individuals began to buy their own houses and send for their families. Some were also scared that a new immigration law might put a stop to the entry of dependants. A Sikh bus driver narrates:

> I am a trained graduate teacher from the Punjab. I came in 1963. I did not try for a teaching job . I was told by my friends that it is hard to get in and anyway the pay is poor. I needed money so I first worked in a

foundry and after two years got on the buses as a bus conductor. There was plenty of overtime. I lived simply — saved almost all my pay packet and bought a big terraced house in 1967. I sent for my family soon after. I have five children, wife and my own mother. Life became more settled after. At least I had cooked meals. Soon after my wife started working in a clothes factory as a machinist.

Anwar's book 'The Myth of Return' gives a picture of Muslim married life.

The whole life-style has changed. He had two children and spent his spare time with his family. His wife, who was a nurse in Pakistan, helped other Pakistani women to write and read letters ... It appeared that at first she missed her parents very much and used to cry a lot ... But after three years she felt settled in the community (Anwar, 1979:193)

Shaw's research shows that the Muslims in Oxford started sending for their families in the mid-1960s and the arrival of women and children can therefore be viewed in terms of putting an end to activities which threatened the values and intentions of Kin in Pakistan (Shaw, 1988: 50).

## Formation of Gurudawaras, Mosques and Temples

For the Asians religion is very much part and parcel of their lives. Believers would like to think that religion guides their daily lives in a practical way. As the communities grew in inner city areas like Handsworth, Wolverhampton, Small Heath and Springbrook they organised themselves along religious and caste affiliations and started to raise funds to acquire places of worship. A foundry worker relates this story:

A committee was formed in (1957) to raise funds for starting a Gurudawara in an old church the first in Smethwick. They knew almost everybody. The committee decided that a week's wages should be the minimum donation they should ask for. That way they raised enough cash to buy the old building.

Likewise Muslim and Hindu communities raised funds to start Mosques and Temples in the Birmingham area. These places of worship soon became foci for cultural, social and political activities; sometimes to the detriment of religious observances. A Sikh comments:

Gurudawara was open every Sunday for 'Bhog' ceremonies. There was 'Shabad Kirtan' (hymn singing) and recitation of Guru Granth Sabib.

The atmosphere was just like back at home. There was an occasional wedding. We also started a 'langar' (free communal kitchen) and later Sunday school for the teaching of Punjabi. But then it was used by the 'Akalis' and 'Congress Wallahs' for their political propaganda ... Also we used to have visiting dignitaries from India to raise funds for hospitals and schools. Recently (1985 onwards) it became terribly politicised because the Golden Temple was attacked by the Indian Army.

A Hindu teacher comments:

We opened Gita Bhavan in the old church in the Ladypool area in 1967. Statues of Lord Rama, Sita, Krishna and other deities had to be brought from India (Jodhpur). Also we managed to get a Brahmin as a priest. Our temple is also a centre for social and cultural activities. We have provision for free meals on Sunday. We have a lot of visiting holy men and women from India and elsewhere for 'Katha' (special sermons). We also teach Hindi to the youngsters twice a week.

Thus the places of worship became a 'defining' factor for the religious communities. As a consequence the communities became well knit, clearly differentiated along the lines of religious affiliations and in moments of crisis could mobilise their members for effective action.

Likewise in Vancouver Sikh Gurudwaras became the centre of religious, social and political activities.

## Values and Belief Systems

There is an interesting school of thought held by anthropologists and social psychologists which differentiates Eastern and Western societies on a bi-polar dimension of collective versus individual orientation (Kluckholn & Strodbeck, 1961; Triandis, 1991; Witkin & Berry, 1975).

Group-orientated people view achievement for group's sake, emphasise co-operation, endurance, order and self-control. Whereas individually-orientated people perceive achievement for self-glory, believe in competition and self-exhibition and pursuit of power.

Triandis (1991) goes on to describe other differences between the two 'types' on norms, values, attitudes and social behaviour which have been supported by cross-cultural researches.

The collective orientation implies, amongst other features, groups as basic units. Others' behaviour reflecting norms and self is defined in terms of in-groups and achievement for the group's sake. Though all societies contain certain elements of collective and individualistic tendencies, the over-riding orientation of traditional societies is towards the collective domain. Thus we have a sound rationale backing the findings of our field-work.

Asian communities are composed of people of different religions, castes, regional and language groups with a variety of social and cultural characteristics. There are, however, certain factors which characterise South Asians as a distinctive group from the Westerners. Firstly there is a primacy of family over the individual as we have already heard from the parents we interviewed.

A typical comment from a Sikh clerical officer:

> I had a job as a clerk, it was a good job with bright prospects. But I could not save much. I had three young sisters at school — for them my parents had to raise dowries. Though we had a small farm it was a hand to mouth existence. I came to England in 1965 after obtaining a voucher. I got an unskilled job in a factory. I saved money to help my family. My three sisters got education, were married with dowries and the family built a 'pukka' (brick built) house. I had a chance to do BSc (Econ) but my family responsibilities came before my self advancement. I had to sacrifice my career for the family but I don't regret it.

Such stories were narrated by all but one of our respondents. This singular exception is a young man who came to study and had no outstanding family responsibilities. Parekh (1986: 198) argues that for the Indians, it is the family rather than the individual which is the basis of social structure. According to another scholar (Buchignani, 1985: 127) 'the family held land, provided most of the labour to work it and shared in the results of labour. It was also a political unit: individuals were weak but households were strong.' Muslim families have a similar role to those of the Hindus and Sikhs.

For the British it is the individual who matters most. It is the individual's feelings, ambitions and potentialities which are paramount and should take precedence over the family. The major aim of education, according to eminent scholars, is the development of autonomy in children. Such a philosophy is often interpreted by Asian parents as leading to 'selfish' children. Here is a comment from a Sikh parent:

> In this country the children are encouraged to be independent to the point of selfishness. They talk back and are rude to their parents. If the parents question their children they respond 'It's none of your business'.

No doubt such over simplified and selective perceptions (stereotypes) are inaccurate but regrettably a large number of Asian parents hold such views about white children and tend to reject Western ideas.

Secondly, religion plays a more important role in the lives of South Asians. Of course, there are class and regional differences, but, by and large, the influence of religion is very strong especially amongst the Muslims. A Muslim commented:

> We want to follow the teaching of the holy Koran and Sharia books; pray five times a day, engage in alms giving, do Haj, and observe Ramadan. According to our religion women should dress modestly and look after home and children. We don't want them to mix with men and flaunt their sex.

For the Hindus it is important to carry on the tradition of vegetarianism, non-violence and a deep spiritual outlook. The Sikhs would like to preserve both the visible symbols (turbans, beards etc.) and the basic teachings of Guru Nank Dev.

In a paradoxical way the Gurudwaras and Hindu temples also reinforced the institutions of caste — which is still a very important differentiator in the Indian and Muslim communities. A Sikh commented:

> Now we have Gurudwaras along caste lines; Jats (Farmer class) were the first followed by Ramgarias (Carpenters) and lastly the Chamars (Harijans) all have separate places. What's the use? The Guru forbade caste distinctions but it has crept back in our religion.

Shaw (1988: 85) also found that caste distinctions are widely used as a basis for invitation to marriages, 'Khatimini Quran' (recitations of the Koran) and other social events, by the Muslim community in Oxford, though Muslims are forbidden to practice a caste system. A Chamar (Harijan) related his experience:

> I was thrown out of a Gurudwara because of my caste. They were alright till they found out I was a Chamar. I used to go out with a Jat girl. Her parents found out and put a stop to it. So when I talk to my white mates about racism they throw this back at my face. They have read about the pernicious effects of the caste system in India.

Now we have a comment from a Sikh factory worker on his religion

> I was advised to shave off my beard and cut my hair when I came to the United kingdom in 1958. I refused. I had a hard time getting a job. Then a friend of mine helped me as I had no English either. I have worked in the same company for thirty years — had no problem with my beard and turban. It is part of my religion. I say my prayers every day and go to the

Gurudwara on Sunday. The teachings of Guru Nanak are simple: believe in one God; salvation achieved through hard work and worship; fellowship with other human beings; no caste system and equality of men and women. These are universal values. Regrettably my boys are clean shaven but my daughter shows more faith. All are university graduates and have been affected by English beliefs.

## Arranged Marriages

The custom of the arranged marriage is very much part and parcel of the Asian social structure. Marriages are supposed to be primarily for the union of families (to promote mutual financial and social interests). But in the Muslim tradition they also reinforce the existing bonds of the extended family as marriages are often arranged between first and second cousins.

Individual wishes, feelings, sentiments and love are considered secondary to the interest of the family, following the widespread belief that 'love comes after marriage'. Here we have the comment of a Sikh woman from Vancouver.

I believe in this custom — otherwise what would our 'Bhai-chara' say — they have become 'Goras' (whites)! Our customs will pass on to the next generation — Punjabi languages, our food, dress and music. Otherwise there won't be anything left of us and people at home will be shocked and terribly disappointed. Also our marriages last longer than Goras — all we hear is a lot of them get divorced in so called 'love marriages'.

This issue causes more problems than any other between the first and the second generation. For the first generation their very survival and ethnic identity depends on it, whilst for most young people it is a matter of individual choice. Though these extreme positions seem irreconcilable a solution is emerging which I shall discuss in subsequent chapters.

## The Position of Women

It may be controversial to make a generalised statement that the majority of the first generation Asian men regard the women's place as being in the home. Regrettably however, in my view, this does describe the attitude of Asian men quite accurately, though there were (and are) social class, religious, caste and regional differences on this issue. Two books (Wilson, 1978; Shan, 1986) describe the situation vividly through biographical narratives. An account given by a Sikh housewife from Birmingham is revealing:

> Firstly I was 'gulam' (slave) to my father's wishes, followed by my broth-
> ers', then my husband's and after his death my sons'. When will I be free?
> We are human beings too! Men have tea, beer, gossip, laugh and joke in
> their spare times, but us .... too busy cooking, cleaning, washing, looking
> after children and entertaining guests. In some cases we are also beaten up
> by the 'Junglis' (savages).

However the experiences of Hindu women are not as grim as the above
comments. A Hindu teacher from Vancouver:

> We have had hard times when we are newly married; not from our hus-
> bands but from our mothers-in-law. When our sons grow up and mothers-
> in-law are gone then we become real 'mistresses of the house'. We take
> care of money, relationships, temple worship, arrangement of marriages
> etc. Even our husbands begin to respect us and start calling us 'mother' of
> our children.

The role of women in Hindu society is thus quite complex. In Hindu the-
ology the female goddesses (Durga, Kali, Sarsawati) are full of 'Shakti' (power
and energy), though they are consorts of over arching Gods of Creation
(Brahama), Preservation (Vishnu) and Destruction (Shiva) respectively. The
Goddess Kali, the consort of Shiva, is widely worshipped by Hindus all over
India. In North America and Britain women have fought hard to secure parity
with men in jobs, promotion, pay-scales and the like. Second-generation Asian
girls, who have socialised into British culture and attitudes through schooling,
are finding it very difficult to reconcile the conflicting demands of home and
school on the gender issue. We shall explore this issue in greater depth in the
next chapter.

## Language Difficulties

The majority of the first-generation immigrants were from a rural background (Dhayna, 1972). A significant number had only attended primary schools
and were completely unaware of the language problems they were going to face
in Britain and Canada. Even with their best efforts (sign language and a few
words) they were misunderstood, caricatured in comedy shows (Peter Sellars'
accent, 'Mind your Language') and generally disapproved of by the indigenous
whites. A comment by a Muslim factory worker from Birmingham illustrates
this.

> The real big problem was language 'Bat'. I felt helpless, a fool and terribly

confused. I was like a deaf person. I got a job through my friends and everything was to be done through this English-speaking boy. That is why I stayed with my relatives. Got on the same bus, bought 'ration' (food) from the same shop and that was it. 'Gaffer' (foreman) could speak few words of Urdu. Ya Allah! how much I suffered. Now my children can speak English — the danger is they won't speak our language. But it was hard to go to the doctor or hospital. When it came to buying my house I was entirely at the mercy of this young boy. Then we had to pay bills — those were terrible times.

Women found it even more difficult to cope with day-to-day living in the early days of settlement. A Hindu woman from Birmingham:

I joined my husband in 1967 along with kids. We came in January. It was very cold. But kids 'pitta ji' (her husband) lit a coal fire so it was alright. The real 'Khasum nu Khani' (damn) problem was English. I was like a deaf-mute, couldn't do shopping, talk to the milkman or go to the doctor. My husband had to take me everywhere — who spoke English. A short while after a lady from the university came to my house once a week to teach me English. 'Jhindi Rahe' (May she live long) she taught me a lot in two years. Then I went to her house once a week for six months. Still now I find it difficult to explain my ailments to the specialist. My angina was not diagnosed — he said it was arthritis — that wretched language has caused me so much distress. I don't fully understand TV programmes and still can't read English newspaper.

## Prejudice and Discrimination

Asians met discrimination in all walks of life. They were mostly given those jobs which were not liked or done by the indigenous whites. They often lived in run-down inner city areas and were generally disapproved of by the host community. Here is the comment of a Hindu bus conductor from Birmingham:

Though I had an MA in History the only job I could get was as a bus conductor. There were a lot of Asians in this work at that time (1960s). After a few years service I applied to a vacant post of wage clerk in the transport department. I had a flat refusal. At job our white mates always used to talk negatively about us. We got overtime only if whites refused to do it. I used to get very upset — but what could you do? You are in their country uninvited. We have also to put up with racial taunts and insults from passengers at night. Several of us got assaulted.

Likewise qualified teachers from India and Pakistan had to face a lot of problems in securing teaching jobs. Partly it was to do with their written and spoken English. Here is an extract from a woman teacher in Birmingham.

My qualifications were not recognised by the DES — though I had taught in the Punjab for several years. I had to attend a special course at Nottingham University to top up my qualification. Even after that I was appointed on a temporary basis — year to year. As regards promotion to higher grade it was impossible I was a 'Paki' and a woman.

Most of the subjects narrated stories of racial harassment and discrimination but there are a few examples where they received generous help from whites. A lecturer explained:

I would say my headmaster was kinder than my father. He helped me with my English, professional development and invited me to his house many times. He gave me very good references and I got on ...

However stories of racial prejudice and discrimination are validated by the researches undertaken by the Policy Studies Institute (Brown, 1984). The author summarised the situation:

First it is clear that racialism and direct racial discrimination continue to have a powerful impact on the lives of black people. Secondly, the position of black citizens of Britain largely remains, geographically and economically, that allocated to immigrant workers in the 1950s and 1960s.

## The Second Generation

Thus, to sum up, most of our respondents were reasonably satisfied with their positions in Britain and Canada. Their aspirations were modest, and they had realised most of their pressing needs; namely finding a job, owning a house and uniting their families in their country of domicile. As regards their interaction with the host community, it was at a minimal level for a number of reasons — language difficulties and lack of familiarity with the customs and practices of the host society being the two main ones.

In Britain the position of the first generation is summarised succinctly by Rex & Tomlinson (1979: 207).

The range of jobs occupied by West Indians and Asians, though it does not overlap substantially with that of the white British living in the area is in fact concentrated more in the lower reaches of the occupational system.

Though the immigrants may join their unions and even express satisfaction with them the likelihood is that the Asians at least would be concentrated in 'black workshops' and 'black shifts' doing dirty tedious and laborious work, relatively cut off from white work-mates and, in times of trouble, under-protected by their unions. They work longer hours for the money they earn and do more shift work. Both groups have been cornered in the system of housing allocation and rely upon systems of credit, buying and rental of abnormal kinds (e.g. council mortgages, housing association tenancies). Their houses, apart from the council houses which some of them live in, are the worst houses in the city which have not yet been demolished even though they are eligible for, and to some extent have benefited from improvement grants. Their children go to primary and comprehensive schools which are largely segregated or are, at least, immigrant majority schools. In these schools they are held back by linguistic and cultural difficulties to which teachers tend to react in terms of cultural stereotypes.

Asian communities have also been adversely affected by the recent recession; unemployment has soared (in Handsworth and Small Heath it is well over 30%) and a large number of small Asian businesses have gone under.

In Canada the position of the Asian communities until the mid-sixties was similar to that of the Asians in Britain; but significant steps have been taken by the Federal Government since the early 1960s to encourage the development of a multicultural society (Anderson & Frideres, 1981: 314). The government pledged to provide support:

First, resources permitting, the government will seek to assist all Canadian cultural groups that have demonstrated a desire and effort to continue to develop a capacity to grow and contribute to Canada, and a clear need for assistance, the small and weak groups no less than the strong and highly organised. Second, the government will assist members of all cultural groups to overcome cultural barriers to full participation in Canadian Society. Third, the government will promote creative encounters and interchange among all Canadian cultural groups in the interests of national unity. Fourth, the government will continue to assist immigrants to acquire one of Canada's official languages in order to become full participants in Canadian society (House of Commons Debates, 1971).

The first Canadian minister of state responsible for multiculturalism was appointed in 1972. The Federal Government also created the Canadian Consultative Council on Multiculturalism in 1976 to set the right climate for tolerance, intercultural understanding and harmony.

Altogether this has improved the conditions of South Asians in Vancouver and elsewhere in Canada. The South Asian communities are quite well off with low unemployment, high property ownership and have actively organised themselves to exert influence in main stream politics.

Whatever their economic and social position, the first generation were and are firmly rooted in their religion and culture and are sure of their personal identities. Their 'belongingness' is not in doubt; they are Sikhs/Muslims or Indians and Pakistanis (Stopes-Roe & Cochrane, 1990).

However, children of these immigrants are less sure of their personal and social identities. They have been described by academics and others as a halfway generation (Taylor, 1976), a generation suffering from 'culture clash' (Thompson, 1974) or youngsters who have the best or worst of the two worlds (Ghuman, 1991). Rex & Thomlinson (1979) have described their situation as 'from immigrants to ethnics'.

By the mid 1970s two out of every five British Asian children were born in this country (Fryer, 1984). This percentage is by now well over 95% (see next chapter), as primary immigration virtually ceased in 1971. The vast majority of children entering British primary schools are now 'third generation' (personal communication from a Birmingham headteacher, 1991).

However, the majority of boys and girls in secondary schools are still from the second generation, both in Birmingham and Vancouver. Their chief problems centre on bridging the gap between the culture of the home and the school (Anwar, 1978; Ghuman, 1975).

The schools reflect the values and belief systems of the host society which, in certain personal and social domains, are at variance with the values of the South Asian homes. At the primary school level there is a discontinuity of customs and practices relating to religious observance, food, dress, manners, language use, types of play and visual signals. At the secondary level, when boys and girls normally become more questioning of all forms of authority, the rift between home and school can begin to appear as a chasm. This is mainly related to 'gender issues'. Girls invariably ask 'Why are we allowed less freedom than the boys?' and personal autonomy 'This is my life and I want to live it my way'. Parents' exasperated anxieties may be expressed, on the other hand, in three key questions:

(1)   Why won't they answer us in Urdu/Punjabi?

(2)   Why are they ashamed of coming to Gurudwara with us?

(3)   Why are they so individualistic and self-centred?

Teachers do play an important role in this situation. On the one hand, they can be sympathetic to the views of both their students and parents and yet take a neutral stance in counselling their students. On the other hand, they can be very ethno-centric and condemn the Asian parents outright, both implicitly and explicitly, for their outmoded and medieval values on marriage, respect for elders and other such matters. Therefore, it was considered imperative to include teachers of these students in our investigation.

However, in our discussion of the differences between the home and the school we must not forget the common ground between the two institutions. For instance, both stress deferred gratification (forsake your pleasures now, for better times in the future), the need for achievement and respect for learning and knowledge. The goddess Sarsawati personifies some of the virtues of good education for the Hindus.

There is a likelihood of inter-generational conflict over 'going out', having girl/boy friends, the choice of clothes and friends, 'curfew' — coming home by a set time, helping parents in the home and businesses and a range of other matters relating to personal autonomy versus family traditions and solidarity.

These are important issues and they called for further investigation to explore current views on such topics. This book reports the findings of two investigations carried out in Birmingham and Vancouver on the issues and concerns outlined above. Two venues were chosen in order to cross-validate findings and to compare and contrast results. The two cities present slightly different cultural contexts, especially in terms of government support for minority cultures. Both cities have a sizeable population of South Asians, except that there are fewer Muslims in Vancouver where the majority are Sikhs. However, the history of immigration has been similar in both places. The major difference between the two countries is that of political climate. In British Columbia (Canada) there is a positive attitude towards multiculturalism, whereas in England such initiatives have been reversed since the early 1980s (Tomlinson, 1991; Troyna, 1990).

The aims of the research may be outlined as follows:

(1) to explore the attitudes of young people (13–16) to the British/Canadian cultures and their home culture;

(2) to explore the opinions of parents and community leaders on educational and social issues which relate to the adolescents' predicament of living in two cultures;

(3) to explore the opinions of teachers and counsellors (Canada only) on the above issues.

As the research is mainly exploratory, rather than being hypothesis based, the sample sizes were small and are summarised in Table 1.2. Another constraint on sample size was the decision to employ the time-consuming, but illuminating, semi-structured interview approach with the sample.

**Table 1.2** Interview samples in Birmingham and Vancouver

| Category | Birmingham | Vancouver | Total |
|----------|------------|-----------|-------|
| Adolescents | 50 | 25 | 75 |
| Parents | 24 | 26 | 50 |
| Community leaders | 6 | 5 | 11 |
| Teachers | 27 | 8 | 35 |
| Home–school link | 1 | 2 | 3 |
| Counsellors | | 4 | 4 |
| | Total respondents | | 178 |

A fuller description of the samples is given in the appropriate chapters but the sample sizes are representative rather than random and were chosen through personal and professional contacts.

## Research Methodology

Being myself South Asian I have a deep understanding of the anxieties and concerns of the families. I lived and taught in Birmingham for twelve years and have visited Vancouver several times in connection with my personal and professional work. It was also advantageous that I was able to converse with the families in Punjabi or Urdu when the need arose. Therefore I am very well aware of the fears of parents, who feel threatened by researchers, journalists and TV and radio interviewers. Here is the response of a Sikh shopkeeper from Birmingham which highlights this anxiety:

> All they are interested in is sensational stuff — how to do the community down, present it as a problem. Show how barbaric and uncivilised their customs and traditions are. They don't want to really understand us — our worries for our kids. We are not jailers — we don't do things for our own ego, but to help our youngsters to grow up in a prejudiced society because they never will be accepted as English because of their colour.

The most suitable method for the collection of information from our samples was through the use of semi-structured interviews. A background questionnaire and an attitude scale were used in addition to the interviews with the adolescents in both national samples. I shall first discuss the semi-structured interview method.

In a semi-structured interview situation although there are a set of questions to be asked and probed into, the order and sequence are largely left to the interviewee. Furthermore, digressions from the main theme are accommodated, and sometimes encouraged, to gain fresh insight into the issues under discussion. Kerlinger (1970: 469) sums it up succinctly:

> the unstandardised, non- structured interview is an open situation in contrast to the standardised, structured interview, which is a closed situation. This does not mean that an unstandardised interview is casual.

There are a number of advantages in using the interview technique over the more structured questionnaire and attitude scale. Firstly, on sensitive topics the interviewer can judge the behaviour of the subjects and monitor the 'questioning' accordingly. Secondly, in-depth questioning can produce rich illuminative information which is not normally possible in a questionnaire. Thirdly, the interviewer can work out fairly accurately whether the subjects are giving reliable (accurate) information. Finally, new perspectives may be revealed on the topics under discussion. For example, when discussing community affairs with the Sikh parents in Vancouver I was told how the community is now taking part in mainstream Liberal party politics and influencing the outcome of the leadership contest — and thus enhancing the importance of the community.

The major weakness of the technique is that it is very time consuming. Therefore only a small representative number can be included in the research. There is also a problem relating to the reliability and accuracy of the data obtained, though this shortcoming is equally applicable to questionnaires. To enhance the reliability of the data it was considered imperative to gain the full confidence of parents, students and teachers.

The following steps were taken to secure the full cooperation of our respondents. In the first place the aims and objectives of our research were made quite clear and the interviewees' minds set at rest concerning my motives and intentions in doing the research. Secondly, complete confidentiality was assured through my personal and professional standing as a long-serving university teacher and researcher. Thirdly, the interviews were conducted in a relaxed and easy manner and, if the interviewee did not wish to respond to any particular question(s), no pressure — subtle or otherwise — was put on them to respond. A related point concerns the use of a cassette recorder during the interview sessions. A number of students (7) refused to have their responses recorded. In this situation detailed notes were taken and the students were re-assured that their conversation would not be repeated or quoted in such a way as to enable them to be identified. The questionnaire used with the students was a straightforward and factual document. They were asked questions on their family religion, language use, community newspapers etc. For details see Appendix 3.

## Construction and Use of Scale

The attitude scale used in the research with young people was constructed by the writer in 1974 (Ghuman, 1975) with a view to assessing the students' opinions on English and their home culture. The scale is named as an acculturation scale, but it is really a bicultural scale, as will become clear from the following details.

The most popular type of scale is constructed along the lines suggested by Likert (1932). Respondents are asked to express their degree of agreement, or otherwise, using a five-point scale for each of a set of statements. The usual procedure is to collect a large number of potential items relating to the topic under investigation. These are then phrased in the form of statements and the long list of statements is reviewed retaining only those that are judged to be clear and addressing a single point. In this case the items relating to British and Asian culture were assembled within the following categories:

(1) those concerned with values and beliefs (e.g. Our customs and traditions are best for us;)

(2) those concerned with leisure and entertainment (e.g. We should visit English cinemas/theatres;)

(3) Those relating to community life (e.g. We should live in our own community;)

(4) those relating to food and clothes (e.g. I would rather eat our own food all the time;)

(5) those relating to the roles of girls and women (e.g. Girls and boys should be treated the same.)

Altogether some 94 items were presented to a group of 16 referees (eight Asians and eight indigenous whites) for their comments as to whether the items genuinely reflected the core values of the two cultures. After taking into consideration the referees' comments 20 items relating to Asian culture and twenty items relating to English culture were selected for a small pilot study. This study utilised a group of ten 15–16-year-old Asian pupils and was used mainly to determine the language difficulty of the items. Six items were rejected as a result of this trial and the remaining 34 items were used for the next pilot stage. For this stage 86 boys and girls, aged 14–16, from two Birmingham schools were asked to complete this 34 item scale. Item analysis of the responses was carried out using standard procedures (Likert, 1932) and it was finally decided to retain 30 items. Some of these were linguistically modified in the light of the comments received from the students and their teachers.

Of the 30 items retained 14 relate to opinions on Asian culture (phrased in such a way as to allow for sub-cultural variations) and 16 to probe attitudes to English customs and practices. Some items are deliberately phrased negatively to break any 'mental set'( i.e. a positive or negative attitude to the scale) which students might develop after reading a number of consistently worded statements. For example 'We should ignore our own language if we want to get on in this country' or 'I would not like our women to behave like English women'. The technical details of the scale are to be found in Appendix 7 but suffice it to say that it has proved to be highly consistent (reliable) and accurate (valid). Evidence on this is presented in Chapter 2.

The scale was finally used for research in the same Birmingham schools as our present sample comes from. Therefore, we have a basis for comparison of the attitudes of the 1974 group with those of 1987. Other scholars (Weinreich, 1983; Berry, 1990) have devised and successfully used scales for assessing acculturation attitudes. The scale was slightly adapted for Canadian use as some of the items derived for Britain are not applicable to the Canadian young people. For instance there is no provision for school meals in Canada. This item was replaced with another school item 'Schools should accept our traditional clothes'. Again statistical analysis showed that the modified version was equally valid as a research instrument.

It was also considered desirable to modify Item 4 slightly following the suggestion from a referee for the NFER that 'going back' could be interpreted as simply going for a holiday. The revised version read 'I have no wish to go back to live in the country where my parents came from'. Following the work in Birmingham, Item 3 was considered to be too general and was replaced by 'We should attend our places of worship'.

## Scoring

To facilitate analysis, items are scored from 5 to 1; 5 for strongly agree, 4 for agree etc. The scoring on Asian items reflecting Asian values is reversed so that discussion becomes more intelligible. Thus, overall, the higher the numerical score obtained the greater the acculturation level attained. The items scored in reverse direction are denoted with an asterisk in Appendices 1 and 2.

Thus if a student were to accept family values and reject all the norms of British/Canadian culture he/she would have a total score of 30. On the other hand if he/she were to accept British/Canadian norms and reject those of the family then the total score would be 150. The total score of any student will be reflective of his/her attitude towards both his/her own family culture and that of British/Canadian culture. This analysis is enhanced when it is combined with family background data collected on the same form as the attitude scale. Furthermore, detailed analysis of the pattern of scores for each item would provide a detailed picture of the students' attitudes.

The next chapter 'Young People Speak Out' presents the evidence obtained by using the scale and interview data. Chapter 3 deals with teachers' attitudes, Chapters 4 and 5 report parents' and communities' concerns respectively on a range of social and educational issues. Finally, in Chapter 6 I have tried to summarise the emerging patterns of ethnic identity, educational issues and biculturalism in general.

# 2 Young People Speak Out

> He has English friends, eats English food and dislikes chappati and curries, his interests are all English. He doesn't want me to wear Indian clothes when I go to his school, he checks everything before his white friends come into our house. Now a black moustache is appearing on his face and he goes: 'What is all this black stuff'. I think he is in for a big shock because whites won't fully accept him. Now my daughter is different. She likes Indian things and feels quite at ease with being Indian and English. (Sikh mother from Birmingham)

This chapter reports the planning and findings of research carried out by the writer in Britain and Canada on Asian youngsters of age 13–16. The main aims of this investigation were two-fold: to ascertain youngsters' attitudes to acculturation (defined as the degree to which they are taking up the norms and values of the British or Anglo-Celtics), and to know the youngsters' opinions on a range of social and educational matters which have a bearing on their personal and social identities.

Before we embark on a lengthy discussion of the contexts and procedures, it is important to place the research in its socio-psychological perspective. Adolescence is a stage between the world of childhood and that of adulthood. It is comparatively short in traditional societies, but in modern technological societies, where high levels of skills are becoming essential for job requirements, it can last for several years. It is a preparatory stage for becoming an adult member of a society with full civic, legal and economic rights and responsibilities.

Adolescence is a period of rapid physical, social and mental development. Physiological changes at puberty result in boys and girls becoming conscious of their developing bodies. Interest in the opposite sex begins to develop and is overtly expressed, at least in the European social milieu. Youngsters begin to take an active interest in 'how they look' and how they present themselves to their peers, teachers and others at school and in the neighbourhood. They begin to take great care in their choice of clothes, hair style, jewellery and the music they listen to. This can lead to arguments and sometimes may be construed by the parents as a challenge to their authority.

Although boys and girls become more prone to peer group influences and pressures, they still seek assurance from their parents about their body image and personal anxieties. This early period of adolescence (12–14 years) is marked by dependence on others.

Intellectually young adolescents begin to show maturity in their thinking processes. They begin to deal with more abstract ideas, and the school curriculum and teaching methods stimulate them to be more independent in their thinking, and more questioning and enquiring in their attitudes. This development often leads them to question parental authority over such matters as bed times, TV viewing, staying out late (or 'curfew' as it is called in North America), choice of friends and clothes, and the playing of loud music.

Sometimes, in late adolescence (16+), such a questioning attitude results in challenging the established authorities of the police, the church (Temples, Gurudwaras or Mosques) and government. Again some adolescents begin to show care and concern over such matters as 'the greenhouse effect', Third World poverty, homelessness in cities and the plight of the elderly. Others may express their dissent through destructive activities — gang fights, alcohol abuse, 'hotting', drug taking and the harassment of minority groups. Thus the adolescence can be a period of minor disagreement, conflict or sometimes major revolt against figures of authority depending on the family, the neighbourhood and the wider social and political climate. All in all, this period can be full of conflict, anxiety and anguish, but most adolescents pass through it without major upheavals (Peterson, 1988).

A related area of concern to adolescents is the world of work. Questions such as 'What are you going to do when you leave school?' loom large by the age of 15. Often the subject choices are made at 13 which strongly influence and constrain the choices in employment. Decisions taken at this stage regarding school-leaving, choice of subjects, exams taken and apprenticeship schemes entered into, often have a lasting impact on later life-styles and status in the adult world. Succinctly, neo-Freudians have summed up adolescence as a period to explore: how to love? and how to work? (Kroger, 1989).

All these changes in body, mind and emotions have important implications for the re-formation of personal and social identities, viz: Who am I? and Who do I belong to? The quest for personal identity, according to Erickson (1968), is a lifelong endeavour, but adolescence is a crucial period of building upon childhood identity. Personal identity is partly dependent on gender and social identities. Social identity is often affirmed during this period through belonging to one or more peer groups which may be along ethnic lines or based on interests such as sports, music or a mixture of many elements. For the purpose of this book it is important that we discuss briefly the ethnic dimension of identity formation.

Ethnic awareness, according to researchers in Britain and elsewhere (Davey *et al.*, 1983), first dawns on children around the age of four and becomes clearly established by approximately seven. However, by the age of 10, according to Davey *et al.* 'it appears, very few children are unaware of the principal attributes of social divisions in societies and most of them are able to verbalise the ones on which their judgements are based' (p. 173). Children entering the adolescent stage are fully aware of their ethnic origins and the esteem and value which are accorded them by the dominant group.

A question may be posed at this juncture: why is it more problematic for an Asian ethnic minority adolescent to form his/her social identity as compared with a white peer? There are, in fact, a number of crucial differences between the white youngsters and the Asians. Firstly, the latter experience overt and covert forms of racial discrimination in schools, jobs and other walks of life and are generally regarded unfavourably by the host society. Secondly, it is not possible for them to identify themselves completely with the whites because of their colour and other visible features, even if they wish to do so. Thirdly, Asian families wish to retain distinctive elements of their cultures; namely, religion, language and endogamous marriages, in order to maintain and reinforce their respective ethnic identities. It is easier for white youngsters to form their social identities when home and school values are more in accord with each other and when society, by and large, is less anxiety-provoking and threatening.

But this process of identity formation may lead to role confusion (not clear about their position in society) in the Asian adolescents as they try to reconcile the discordant values and norms of their family with that of the school. Yet, on the other hand, they may successfully synthesise the values of the two cultures and develop a life-style, with the support of their peer group, and become bicultural in outlook, i.e. develop bicultural identity. According to Rosenthal (1986: 179), 'the evidence seems to suggest that the integration of two cultural worlds can be an enriching experience yielding flexible individuals with skills that enable them to function adaptively in a variety of contexts'. Crucial to the successful outcome of living in two cultures is the positive evaluation and healthy attitudes of the dominant group towards the minority ethnic group. I shall explore this dimension in our discussion of the research undertaken in two socio-political contexts with differing attitudes to ethnic minorities.

As the family exerts a major influence on the identity development of adolescents, it is important to discuss the major differences between the indigenous white families and the Asian families. There are two differences of importance: attitude to sex and women, and the authoritarian structure of the family. Pre-marital sex and courtship are strictly forbidden in Asian communities. Asian youngsters are not given the same degree of freedom as is allowed to the whites to explore relationships with the opposite sex. In some orthodox Muslim families, girls are separated from the boys at puberty (and only allowed male contact with very close family members). Love is supposed to come and grow after marriage — a complete reversal from the Western pattern. Most Asian parents are more protective towards their daughters and allow them less freedom as compared with boys; though there are class, religious and regional differences on this matter. I shall explore this in my subsequent discussion.

The second important difference lies in the structure of the family. Asian families tend to be patriarchal and authoritarian. Fathers are the head of the family, and the chief decision-makers, particularly in Muslim and Sikh communities. Hindus do have a 'power-sharing' attitude and some scholars comment that Hindu women have effectively more power than men (Singh, 1966). Generally speaking, as compared to the modern Western family, the youngsters come pretty low down in the family hierarchy, especially when they happen to be girls (Wilson, 1978). Therefore, the communication pattern, level of participation and decision making are somewhat different from the Western pattern.

According to some scholars (Parekh, 1986; Triandis, 1991) it is the family and not the individual which is the basic unit in Asian communities. The individual's wishes and desires have to be harmonised with that of the family. Individual development as understood and aimed for by the Western educationalists is interpreted as leading to selfishness and egomania by the Asian Community. Often the individuals are expected to sacrifice themselves for the sake of the family traditions, honour (Izzat) and welfare. The chain immigration in the 1960s demonstrates this clearly. A male member of the family supported his extended family back in Pakistan for several years, and also made arrangements for his brothers, and other relatives, to join him in England.

There is yet another difference between the Western and the Asian parents in that most of the former probably have experienced the pain and joys of going through the adolescent period (popular books, 'The Diary of Adrian Mole', for instance, illustrate this vividly), but most of the Asian parents, who are predominantly from a rural background, have little experience of being in between the stages of childhood and adulthood. Most left primary and lower secondary school and went to work on their family farms or took up the trades of their parents or kinsfolk. There were few choices and, anyway, decisions were mainly made by the fathers. However, parents from urban backgrounds are more aware and appreciative of adolescents' concerns and anxieties in the Western context.

The school culture in Britain and Canada predominantly reflects the Anglo-Saxon and Western European cultures. School curricula are extremely Euro-centric and scant attention is paid to the contributions of the Hindus, the Chinese and the Egyptians to the growth of human civilisations. Most white teachers are ethno-centric (especially in Britain) and still believe in assimilating minorities into the mainstream British/Canadian cultures.

Therefore, Asian youngsters have to learn to live with two cultures: one of the home and the other of the school. The purpose of this research was to explore the views of youngsters, teachers and counsellors and community leaders on issues which are relevant and important to the education and identity formation of Asian adolescents who were born and educated in Britain and Canada but who are still influenced by their families' traditions and values.

## Research Contexts

### Britain

I selected three multicultural schools in Birmingham for this research, the chief reason being that I had a longstanding contact of over 20 years with them. I had extensively used the three schools for our teacher trainee students, honours students and for small-scale research projects. Therefore, I was deeply acquainted with the history and the ethos of the schools and the neighbourhood communities.

Asian communities have developed distinctive identities through close family and kinship ties, endogamous marriages, links with 'home countries', temples, Gurudwaras and Mosques, and community centres. They have established weekend schools in their places of worship for the teaching of home languages. Special food, jewellery and textile shops have come into existence because of the demands for things Indian or Pakistani. The settlement of the ethnic groups is very much along the religious and kinsfolk lines. One locale is predominantly inhabited by Sikhs and Hindus and the other mainly by Muslims. There is a sprinkling of Afro-Caribbeans, but the vast majority of whites have left the areas. The locales, therefore, have become almost ethnic enclaves for the Asian communities.

The schools reflect the ethnic composition of the areas — over 90% of students are Asians, 5% blacks and around 5% whites. The staff in all three schools are white with the exception of a few Asian and black teachers. In two schools a senior position was held by a non-white person.

All three schools have implemented a type of multicultural education policy. All have multi-religious assemblies, girls are allowed to wear a modified form of school uniform, if they so wish. There is provision for ethnic meals at lunch time, physical education classes are held separately and Urdu or Punjabi is taught within the schools' curricula. Parents are represented on the governing bodies and schools foster active links with the local community.

These schools have reasonable facilities for teaching and extra-curricular activities, but one 'opt out' school has excellent facilities for teaching computing, drama and music.

The attitude of the senior staff to multicultural education is lukewarm and can be summarised in the following quotations:

(1)  'If only they would speak English at home';

(2)  'What is the use of Punjabi? They are going to live in England not in Pakistan';

(3)  'They should learn our ways; they could learn their own language at home'.

As regards multicultural curriculum innovation, it is sadly lacking. But there are some examples of innovation in History and Geography teaching. The whole process of multiculturalism has virtually come to a halt with the introduction of the National Curriculum. However, according to the headmaster of one of the schools: 'Parents approve of the traditional curriculum and examination-orientated approach and we don't want to dilute our teaching with trendy stuff'. The schools' curricula are very much still Euro-centric.

## Canada: British Columbia

The research was carried out in East Vancouver during July, 1989. The area is very much a multi-ethnic one: there are sizeable communities of East Indians/Indo-Canadians (Asians in British terminology), Chinese, Filipinos and whites. The Indo-Canadian community is mainly composed of Sikhs from the Punjab and Hindus from India, Fiji and East Africa. There are virtually no Muslim families in this part of Vancouver.

The Sikhs have maintained their distinctiveness through Gurudwaras, separate shopping centres, community organisations, endogamous marriages and links with Punjab. Likewise, the Hindu community has maintained its identity through similar institutions and practices. The Sikhs, though an established and influential community, went through a difficult period (1984–88) because of the highly explosive events in the Punjab. The operation 'Blue Star' — military action ordered by the late Mrs Ghandi — set off a train of events which were to seriously tarnish and damage the Sikh reputation world-wide. However, the community has restored its previous image of hard-working, tenacious and enterprising people which it enjoyed before the events in the Punjab.

The Vancouver School Board invited four schools to participate in my research. Two schools agreed, subject to the established procedures that I first seek permission from the parents. In the event, I received excellent co-operation from the parents, pupils and teachers.

Both schools are alike in that they have a truly multi-ethnic intake, 1/3 Indo-Canadian, 1/3 Chinese and Filipinos and 1/3 white. Most of the staff are white, with very few exceptions. There are no school uniforms, no morning assemblies and no school dinners. Students are allowed to wear ethnic clothes. But I did not see even a single example of it, except for a couple of Sikh boys wearing turbans. There are separate classes for the newly arrived ethnic students. These students are integrated into the mainstream classes as soon as they achieve a satisfactory level of competence in English.

As regards the rest of the school curriculum, there is provision for the teaching of Mandarin in both schools. Punjabi is taught on the school premises, but after school hours. Multicultural innovations in the school curriculum are in the embryonic stage. Both schools have a broad-based curriculum ranging from Maths to technical drawing through domestic science and secretarial courses. The majority (over 80%) of students stay at school until 18 to graduate. There are excellent library facilities: carpeted floors, with separate booths, and staffed by a full-time Librarian. The libraries must contain in excess of 2000 books and a very large collection of visual aids material, videos, transparencies, films, charts and maps. Likewise, facilities for teaching other subjects are really excellent in comparison with the British schools. The atmospheres of the schools were relaxed, yet educationally effective. Relationships between the teaching staff and students were very informal when compared to the British schools. Somehow youngsters are given more adult-like status.

There are two additional features to note in Vancouver schools; firstly, there are ethnic home–school workers, Punjabi-speaking and Mandarin speaking, and secondly, schools employ counsellors to help, support, and guide students' academic, vocational and personal development. The employment of school counsellors has not taken root in Britain; therefore, the personal and vocational guidance is very much 'ad hoc' as compared with the Canadian Schools.

# Sampling

### Birmingham

The Headteachers were requested to allow access to all the 3rd, 4th and 5th years (13, 14, 15 years old) students of Asian origins to complete an attitude scale on acculturation. In addition I asked for a sample of 20 boys and girls from each school (60 in all) to participate in an in-depth interview. These boys and girls were selected for me by the deputy heads of the schools and were supposed to be representative of age and gender composition of the Asian pupils. In tabulation and analysis I have placed the Hindus and Sikh students in the same category. There are two reasons for this: on the one hand there are not sufficient numbers in separate categories 'for analysis and, on the other hand, the living styles of the two communities are very close indeed. Inter-marriages are accepted and there is a bond of common language and country. The situation in the Punjab has somewhat soured the relations between the two communities in Britain and Canada. Nevertheless they are closer in polity, attitudes and values as compared with the Muslims.

First, I shall present the sample details of boys and girls who supplied the background information and completed the attitude scale in Tables 2.1 to 2.3. Table 2.4 gives information on those who were interviewed.

In the interviews the initial aim was to obtain equal numbers in the two main categories (Hindus and Sikhs, and Muslims) but due to malfunctioning of the tape-recorder and diffidence shown by some students, the final figures are short of the original target. 84% of boys and girls were born in this country, but all of them had primary schooling in England except one Hindu girl whose father was an official in the Indian Commissioner's Office.

**Table 2.1** Religion, country of birth and school attended in the UK

|  | Born in UK | Primary schooling | Muslims | Hindus and Sikhs* | Others** | Total N |
|---|---|---|---|---|---|---|
| Boys | 170(65) | 241(92) | 154(59) | 92(35) | 16(6) | 262 |
| Girls | 160(79) | 182(90) | 55(27) | 134(66) | 14(7) | 203 |

\*    Hindus and Sikhs are put together for analysis as both groups were small in number.
\*\*   Includes Christians, Buddhists and Jains.
Numbers in parentheses are percentages.

**Table 2.2** Registrar-General's classification of socio-economic status of sample
— Birmingham

|  | I, II, IIIa | IIIb, IV, V | Unemployed | Missing data and others | Total |
|---|---|---|---|---|---|
| Boys | 40(15) | 65(25) | 92(35) | 65(25) | 262 |
| Girls | 36(18) | 47(23) | 73(36) | 47(23) | 203 |

Numbers in parentheses are percentages.

**Table 2.3** Language spoken at home — Birmingham

|  | English | Asian | Bilingual | No response | Total N |
|---|---|---|---|---|---|
| Boys | 14(5.5) | 19(7.5) | 224(85) | 5(2) | 262 |
| Girls | 7(3.5) | 10(5) | 183(90) | 3(1.5) | 203 |

Numbers in parentheses are percentages.

**Table 2.4** Birmingham sample for interview

|  | Boys | Girls | Total |
|---|---|---|---|
| Hindus + Sikhs | 14 | 16 | 30 |
| Muslims | 11 | 9 | 20 |
| Total | 25 | 25 | 50 |

## Vancouver

The sample which completed the background and acculturation question-naire is smaller than the British sample ($N = 101$). The main reason is that par-ents' consent had to be sought before any testing or questioning of students. The mechanism for doing this is not easy. Additionally, the principal of a Khalsa school (a private Sikh school), and two other principals, refused to participate in the research programme for a variety of reasons. Later I shall discuss the response of the Khalsa school's principal as it sheds light on the identity of Sikh children. The details of the sample are given in Tables 2.5, 2.6, 2.7 and 2.8.

**Table 2.5** Country of birth and school attended in Vancouver.

|       | Born in Canada | Primary school | N  |             |
|-------|----------------|----------------|----|-------------|
| Boys  | 40(81)         | 48(94)         | 51 |             |
| Girls | 40(81)         | 47(93)         | 49 | Total = 100 |

Numbers in parentheses are percentages.

**Table 2.6** Religious composition of the sample — Vancouver

|       | Hindus | Sikhs | Total |
|-------|--------|-------|-------|
| Boys  | 12     | 39    | 51    |
| Girls | 11     | 38    | 49    |
| Total | 23     | 77    | 100   |

**Table 2.7** Language spoken at home (%) — Vancouver

|               | English | Punjabi/Hindi | Bilingual |
|---------------|---------|---------------|-----------|
| Boys & Girls  | 7.5     | 8.5           | 84        |

**Table 2.8** Parents' occupation — Registrar-General's Classification (%) — Vancouver

|         | Non-Manual (I, II, IIIa) | Manual (IIIb, IV, V) | Unemployed | Others No response |
|---------|--------------------------|----------------------|------------|--------------------|
| Fathers | 12                       | 70                   | 7          | 11                 |
| Mothers | 7.6                      | 55.4                 | 37*        | —                  |

*Housework.

It is interesting to note that with the Canadian sample we asked students their mothers' job/work: 63% go out to work — mostly engaged in cleaning jobs, and the rest are housewives, a number of whom would also like to work, should it become available. Most of the fathers are employed in the local saw-mills as manual workers and the non-manual category includes fathers who had their own businesses. The unemployment rate is only 7%, in marked con-trast to the Birmingham sample where it was over 35%. 78% of the sample admits to speaking a mixture of English and Punjabi/Hindi/Gujrati: i.e. a form of bilingualism is practised in most Asian homes. In Birmingham the per-centage was slightly higher — (87%). I shall discuss the implications of this result in our concluding analysis.

For our interview sessions 13 boys and 12 girls agreed to take part; their age range is representative of the larger sample used for the acculturation scale.

The following focused research questions were asked:

(a)   Is there a difference between boys and girls on acculturation?

(b)   Is there any difference between Muslims and Hindus & Sikhs?

(c)   Does socio-economic status make any difference to views on acculturation?

(d)   Is there any difference between our sample of 1974 and the present one (relates to Birmingham sample only)?

(e)   What are the overall views of youngsters on acculturation?

(f)   Is there any difference between the Birmingham sample and the Vancouver sample?

## Analysis and Discussion of the Data from the Acculturation Scale

To remind the reader of our scoring method, it was decided to award a mark of 5 to 'strongly agree', 4 to 'agree', 3 to 'undecided', 2 to 'disagree' and 1 to 'strongly disagree' statements. The scoring was designed in such a way that the high scores on the scale should represent a higher degree of acculturation and vice versa. Therefore the scoring of the items (3, 6, 7, 9, 11, 12, 13, 14, 19, 21, 23, 25, 26 and 29 for Birmingham scale) which showed adherence to home culture, was reversed, i.e. strongly disagree was 5 and disagree 4 and so on. For the scale used in Vancouver the scoring on the following items was reversed (2, 3, 6, 7, 9, 11, 12, 14, 17, 19, 21, 23, 25, 26, 29). First we compared the perfor-mance of our Birmingham sample with an earlier sample collected from the same schools some 13 years ago (see Ghuman, 1975) to find out whether there had been changes in attitude to acculturation. The 1974 sample consisted of 43 boys and 55 girls. Therefore I randomly selected 50 boys and 50 girls from our 1987 sample for a valid comparative analysis.

**Table 2.9** Mean scores and standard deviations of 1987 and 1974 samples

|      | *Boys\** | *Girls\*\** |
|------|----------|-------------|
| 1987 | M=91.20  | M=104.23    |
|      | SD=12.70 | SD=13.61    |
|      | N=50     | N=50        |
| 1974 | M=88.97  | M=99.20     |
|      | SD=13.5  | SD=13.75    |
|      | N=43     | N=55        |

\*t=1.15, df=91 Not significant.
\*\*t=2.63, df=103 Significant at 0.02 level.

Girls of the 1987 sample scored significantly higher than the girls of 1974 sample; boys scored higher but not above chance level. On the whole, the 1987 sample shows a higher degree of acculturation than the 1974 sample, which is to be expected.

For a detailed analysis, I carried out a test of significance on all 30 items to pin-point the differences in cultural outlook. The chi-squared test was used for this purpose. On the following items in Table 2.10 significant differences were found (P=0.05).

Thus our present sample shows a more favourable attitude to English culture and respondents are less in favour of retention of their traditional customs.

## Comparison of Birmingham and Vancouver Samples

Now I shall compare the performance of the Birmingham sample with that of the Vancouver sample. As the Canadian sample is only composed of Hindu and Sikh boys and girls, I will compare only the performance of the Hindu and Sikh students from our Birmingham sample.

Differences in scores between the two groups, treating boys and girls separately, are highly significant and are in favour of the Canadian boys and girls (P<0.05). The inference from the results is clear: Canadian youngsters are more willing to take up the norms of the host culture (see Table 2.11).

**Table 2.10** Comparison of 1987 with 1974 group on selected items % (collapsed categories)

| Items abbreviated | | Strongly agree + Agree | Undecided | Strongly disagree + Disagree | N |
|---|---|---|---|---|---|
| Parents and children should | New | 53 | 15 | 32 | 99 |
| live on their own | Old | 43 | 27 | 30 | 98 |
| A woman's place is in the home | New | 16 | 7 | 77 | 100 |
| | Old | 26 | 9 | 65 | 97 |
| Learn to speak our | New | 67 | 17 | 16 | 98 |
| own language | Old | 89 | 6 | 5 | 98 |
| It is good for us to learn | New | 67 | 19 | 14 | 100 |
| something about Christianity | Old | 47 | 22 | 31 | 98 |
| Should be more inter-marriages | New | 35 | 33 | 32 | 98 |
| | Old | 22 | 23 | 55 | 96 |
| Our women shouldn't behave | New | 29 | 23 | 48 | 98 |
| like the English | Old | 48 | 26 | 26 | 97 |
| Men should make all | New | 18 | 15 | 67 | 100 |
| the decisions | Old | 29 | 14 | 57 | 99 |
| Our women should wear | New | 40 | 29 | 31 | 100 |
| English clothes | Old | 23 | 32 | 45 | 97 |

**Table 2.11** Comparative mean scores of Birmingham and Vancouver samples

| | Boys | Girls |
|---|---|---|
| Birmingham | M=96.45 | M=105.21 |
| | SD=11.37 | SD=12.17 |
| | N=92 | N=131 |
| Vancouver | M=107.06 | M=109.45 |
| | SD=10.98 | SD=16.96 |
| | N=51 | N=49 |

## Gender differences

I shall return to this theme of difference later in our discussion on gender differences. As we can see from Tables 2.10 and 2.11 girls show a more favourable attitude to culture change than boys in both research locales. These differences are significant. In our Birmingham sample girls expressed more favourable attitudes on 16 out of 30 items and boys on the time relating to school dinners, viz: 'we should stay for school dinners'. Girls showed strikingly positive attitudes to items relating to the equality of sexes and to the role of women.

As regards gender differences in the Canadian sample, the pattern is similar to the English sample except that girls are even more conscious of their low status in the Indian community and want equality of treatment with boys.

**Table 2.12** Selected items on which marked differences were found between the boys and girls

|  |  | Strongly agree+ Agree % | Undecided % | Strongly disagree + Disagree % | Total N |
|---|---|---|---|---|---|
| Girls and boys should | G | 97 | 2 | 1 | 203 |
| be treated the same | B | 84 | 5 | 11 | 260 |
| A woman's place | G | 12 | 3 | 85 | 202 |
| is in the home | B | 19 | 16 | 65 | 259 |
| Marriages should | G | 31 | 18 | 51 | 201 |
| be arranged | B | 41 | 22 | 37 | 258 |
| Asian women shouldn't | G | 25 | 24 | 51 | 203 |
| behave like the English | B | 52 | 17 | 31 | 260 |
| Men should make all the | G | 12 | 12 | 77 | 199 |
| decisions of the family | B | 28 | 19 | 53 | 259 |

All differences are significant beyond $p<0.01$; chi-squared was calculated with full five-point scale and four degrees of freedom.

## Socio-economic status

It was speculated that adolescents from non-manual backgrounds would show more willingness to accept lost community norms. Regrettably our

Canadian sample is too small for meaningful comparison; therefore I present only the analysis on the Birmingham sample.

**Table 2.13** Mean scores and standard deviations of non-manual and manual sub-samples

|  | Boys* | Girls** |
|---|---|---|
| Non-manual | M=94.57 | M=105.68 |
|  | SD=10.59 | SD=9.84 |
|  | N=40 | N=36 |
| Manual | M=89.64 | M=101.71 |
|  | SD=13.81 | SD=14.71 |
|  | N=65 | N=47 |

*t=2.89, df=103, P<0.01
** t=2.02, df=81; P<0.05.

The difference between the two classes (boys and girls analysed separately) is significant for girls, and is in the predicted direction. The reasons for this may be manifold, but it is likely to be due to higher educational background and the fact that those in non-manual occupations have wider opportunities to mix with indigenous white groups.

**Religion**

We intend to compare the scores of Muslim boys and girls with those of 'Hindu & Sikh' boys and girls respectively. Our Canadian sample did not have any Muslim students, so we did a comparative analysis on the Birmingham sample.

It is widely accepted that the Muslim communities in the UK, France, Germany and in North America are generally more conservative than Hindus and Sikhs. The Rushdie affair, and more recently some support for Iraq among Muslims, have highlighted this perception. Our item analysis carried out by the use of chi-squared test showed that on all items, except three (21, 22, 23), Hindu and Sikh youngsters showed a more positive attitude to culture change.

**Table 2.14** Mean scores and standard deviations of Muslims and Hindu & Sikh
adolescents — Birmingham sample

|                  | *Boys**       | *Girls***      |
|------------------|---------------|----------------|
| Muslims          | M=86.29       | M=98.12        |
|                  | SD=12.29      | SD=16.34       |
|                  | N=154         | N=56           |
| Hindus & Sikhs   | M=96.45       | M=105.21       |
|                  | SD=11.37      | SD=12.17       |
|                  | N=92          | N=131          |

*t=9.96, df=244; P<0.01
**t=4.76, df=185; P<0.01

It is quite clear from the above data that the Muslim boys and girls are less favourable to culture change.

In order to illustrate class and gender differences more vividly, we compiled a ranking of groups based on their respective average marks on the whole scale (see Table 2.15).

It is interesting to note that girls from non-manual backgrounds, irrespective of their religion, express the most positive attitude to culture change, followed closely by Hindu and Sikh girls. The least acculturated groups are the Muslim boys and boys from the manual class backgrounds. The scale, therefore, has provided a useful and valid ranking order which is confirmed by our deep knowledge of Asian communities. I shall further discuss the group and gender differences along with our interview data.

## General Findings

The pattern which emerged from our data is very interesting indeed. Both samples express their attitudes remarkably consistently and the results show coherence and order, which is illuminating. I shall discuss the findings under the following separate headings: (a) acculturation; (b) retention of home culture; (c) rejection of home cultural norms; (d) ambivalent areas. These four categories fully describe our acculturation scale. These categories emerged from our analysis of the frequency tables which were calculated for each item on the continuum of: strongly agree; agree; undecided; disagree; and strongly disagree. For instance, on the first item, 'Boys and girls should be treated alike', the response pattern was: 90, 5, 2, 3. Therefore the item reflects the positive attitude for equality (which, of course, is as British as a Canadian norm). The cut-off point for inclusion of items was fixed at 66%, i.e. if strongly agree or/and agree categories came to 66% and vice versa. The items which fell in the ambivalence category were those whose response pattern was close to evenly distributed frequencies, i.e. 25%, 25%, 25%, 25%, or where over 30% responses fell in the category of 'undecided'.

**Table 2.15** Group ranking based on numerical scores — Birmingham sample

|                  | Mean   | SD    | N   |
| ---------------- | ------ | ----- | --- |
| *Girls*          |        |       |     |
| Non-manual       | 105.68 | 9.84  | 36  |
| Hindus & Sikhs   | 105.21 | 12.17 | 131 |
| All              | 103.51 | 13.73 | 203 |
| Manual           | 101.71 | 14.71 | 47  |
| Muslims          | 98.12  | 16.34 | 56  |
| *Boys*           |        |       |     |
| Hindus & Sikhs   | 96.45  | 11.37 | 92  |
| Non-manual       | 94.57  | 10.59 | 40  |
| All              | 90.33  | 12.64 | 262 |
| Manual           | 89.64  | 13.81 | 65  |
| Muslims          | 86.29  | 12.29 | 154 |

# Acculturation

Boys and girls from Birmingham and Vancouver show positive attitudes on 'equality of treatment of boys and girls', 'cooking of English/Canadian food at home', 'visiting English/Canadian friends', 'going to English cinemas and play movies', 'choice of clothes', and 'celebrating Christmas as our own festivals'. In addition the Canadian sample also approves of: 'our women should wear European clothes', 'our boys and girls should go out with white Canadian boys and girls'. The Birmingham sample is ambivalent on these items. On the other hand, the Birmingham sample agrees with the claim: 'We should learn something about Christianity', whereas the Canadian is neutral. The possible reason behind this may be that the teaching of religion is not a part of the formal or informal school curriculum in Canada and there are no morning assemblies.

It also emerged from our analyses that the Vancouver sample's responses were more favourable to acculturation as compared with the Birmingham one in intensity, i.e. more ticking, 'strongly agree' category, and frequency.

## Retention of Home Cultural Values

Both samples favour the retention of home language 'very strongly' and support 'fulfilling parents' wishes' — a sign of family loyalty — and the 'retention of their original names', though the Canadian boys and girls are less sure of this. Many Indo-Canadian students have anglicised their names: Surinder, for instance, has easily been adapted to Sue. Some have taken an additional anglicised name, such as David, according to our observation and analysis of the class registers.

The Canadian sample supports 'attending the places of worship', a replacement item on the scale in lieu of the 'school dinner' item. There is no provision for school meals in the Canadian schools.

## Areas of Ambivalence

There were some marked difference between the two samples on this category. Whilst there was common uncertainty on the following: 'Not wishing to go back', 'parents should live on their own', 'inter-ethnic marriages', and 'women behaving like the English/Canadian', the Birmingham sample also had doubts about 'school dinners', 'marriages should be arranged by the family' (rejected by the Canadian sample), 'our customs are best for us', and 'our films are more entertaining than English films'. The Vancouver sample was also ambivalent on 'schools accepting traditional clothes', changing of names' and 'learning something about Christianity'.

## Rejection of Home Cultural Values

The boys and girls from both samples reject items on 'women's place is in the home', 'only our own doctors can understand our illnesses', 'living within one's own community', 'making friends with one's own community', 'cooking one's own food all the time', and 'men should make all the decisions in the family'. In addition, the Vancouver sample also showed unfavourable opinion on: 'arranged marriages' and 'our films are more entertaining'.

It appears from the above analysis that these boys and girls do not wish to be completely submerged in their own ethnic communities. They reject attitudes which are inward looking and lead to segregation — the Canadian more so than the British.

Further discussion of the findings is deferred to the next section where I analyse the new interview schedules. But there are two points which may be borne in mind. First, all youngsters in our samples show favourable attitudes to large areas of English/Canadian culture, whilst relating to elements of their own. Second, the Indo-Canadians show far more positive attitudes towards the Canadian culture to the extent that they are not sure whether they should keep their Asian names.

## Analysis and Discussion of Interview Schedules

As described earlier, 50 boys and girls from Birmingham schools and 25 from Vancouver schools were interviewed to find out their views on a range of personal, educational and social matters. The chief aim was to explore their true feelings, as far as possible, on many sensitive issues: such as arranged marriages, ethnic identity, vocational aspirations and adjustment at school. (The full list appears in Appendix 4.) We have described the details of the interview method, recording etc. in the first chapter but, very briefly, ours were semi-structured interviews and youngsters were asked whether we could tape-record their answers. Several (8/25) Canadian students refused, and in these cases we had to take detailed notes of their responses. Though we had a list of topics to be discussed, they were not taken in any strict order and youngsters were not put under any pressure to answer each and every question put to them. Furthermore, in certain cases (6 Birmingham, 3 Vancouver) we had to terminate our interviews because of the diffidence shown by the subjects. Some students were far more articulate than others, and took longer to inter-view, but generally girls had a lot more to say than boys and older pupils were more confident and expressive of their views. Students were also given the opportunity to ask the researcher any questions they wished on the current research or any other relevant matters. Several boys and girls asked intelligent questions regarding the purpose of research and my personal and social back-ground. My first impression was the striking differences between the Indo-Canadian boys and girls and the British/Asian boys and girls. The former were casually but smartly dressed, very straightforward, confident and sure of themselves. In contrast, Birmingham 'pupils' were dressed in school uniforms, very polite, slightly sceptical and unsure of themselves. Several boys and girls from Vancouver had relatives in Birmingham and elsewhere in Britain and vice versa. Therefore on occasions they did compare the two situations on such things as jobs, opportunities, sports facilities and youth centres.

**Table 2.16** Occupation of parents — Birmingham sample

|  |  | Non-manual | Manual | Unemployed | Household |
|---|---|---|---|---|---|
| Hindus + Sikhs | Father | 5 | 13 | 12 | – |
|  | Mother | 2 | 11 | – | 17 |
| Muslims | Father | 1 | 8 | 11 | – |
|  | Mother | 2 | – | – | 18 |

We have not used the full Registrar-General's classification because of the small numbers likely to result in each of the seven categories.

The data on the Canadian sample are in Table 2.17.

**Table 2.17** Occupation of parents — Vancouver sample

|  | Non-manual | Manual | Unemployed | Household |
|---|---|---|---|---|
| Father | 3 | 19 | 3 | – |
| Mother | 4 | 10 | – | 11 |

There are three important inferences to be drawn from the figures of Table 2.16: 46% of the fathers are unemployed, the majority work in manual jobs, and the fact that more Hindu and Sikh women go out to work as compared to the Muslim samples in Birmingham. The last difference in itself reflects the differing attitudes of the communities to cultural adaptation.

Hindus, in particular, have been very successful in Leicester and elsewhere as the men share responsibilities for running businesses with their womenfolk. The Sikh community is also beginning to emulate their example, but the Muslim community, by and large, is very orthodox on this issue. As far as the Canadian sample is concerned, we see the unemployment rate a lot lower than in the British sample. Ethnic minority communities have been badly affected by the recession in the UK. Their unemployment rate is often twice as high as the indigenous population in most UK cities. Our findings from the interview data are very close to the responses boys and girls gave on the acculturation scale.

**Table 2.18** Number of children and type of family — Birmingham sample

|                | 1–3 | 4–5 | 6+ | No response |
|----------------|-----|-----|----|-------------|
| Hindus + Sikhs | 14  | 6   | 6  | 4           |
| Muslims        | 3   | 5   | 8  | 4           |

Muslim parents still tend to have larger families, and 50% of the total sample have three or more children — indicating a traditional attitude towards large families. In the Vancouver sample, 12/25 have three or more children — a similar pattern to that of the Birmingham sample.

In the Birmingham sample, all the Hindu and Sikh families are nuclear except two, whereas in the Muslim sample 15 are nuclear and five are extended. In the Canadian sample, 18 are nuclear and seven are extended. Overall, we see a clear trend towards the indigenous whites: another sign of adaptation to a British and Canadian norm.

In both samples, when questioned about the nature of the household, students' replies showed that uncles and aunts now live on the same street, rather than in the same household as they used to, and that the grandparents either 'rotate' and live in turn with their sons, and sometimes with daughters, or prefer to live in the warmer climate of India/Pakistan. The reader may be reminded here that 'elderly' Asians are supposed to be the responsibility of the sons rather than the daughters. It would be a social disgrace if the grandparents were to live with their daughters. This is in sharp contrast to the British practice where daughters normally look after their aged parents.

Students' replies to the extended family were along the lines: 'We must look after 'Nana and Baba Js'; after all they have made big sacrifices for the family.'

**Table 2.19** Own room — Birmingham sample

|               | Yes | No  | No response |
| ------------- | --- | --- | ----------- |
| Hindus + Sikhs | 9   | 11  | 10          |
| Muslims       | 6   | 7   | 7           |
| Total         | 15  | 18  | 17 =50      |

30% have their own rooms, 36% share a room with a sibling and 34% refused to answer this question. In the Vancouver sample, 60% had their own rooms, 32% shared a room and 8% did not respond — a pattern which is a lot better than the one found with the Birmingham sample.

From our observations of the Birmingham sample, we inferred that the youngsters not responding to this question were probably too embarrassed to admit that they shared a room, which some of them had to do because of the large family size and generally low household income due to chronic unemployment.

This finding has implications for students' progress at school. It is well established now (Vernon, 1969; Wiseman, 1966) that facilities provided by the home for school work and personal study have an important bearing on academic performance.

**Table 2.20** Food – Birmingham sample

|               | Mainly Indian/Pakistan | Mixed | Mainly English |      |
| ------------- | ---------------------- | ----- | -------------- | ---- |
| Hindus + Sikhs | 22                     | 8     | 0              |      |
| Muslims       | 15                     | 5     | 0              |      |
| Total         | 37                     | 13    | 0              | =50  |

74% of the families cook mainly Asian dishes. A Muslim boy replied: 'Halal meat and chappatis, kebabs and stuff ... I have chips in the evening sometimes.' A Hindu girl: 'Lamb, chicken, English food, sometimes pie and chips ... for them I go down to the Chippies.' Mixed food eaters responded: 'Curry, rice, chips and beans', or 'nothing in the morning, sandwiches from the school or chip shop at dinner time; in the evening, my mum makes chappati sometimes. We have pitta bread'.

As regards the Canadian sample, the majority (15/25) also cook traditional food like the Birmingham sample. A significant number, however, have changed their cooking to a mixed variety — Italian pizzas are popular and so are the Chinese dishes. Here are some interesting replies: 'It is a mixture of both — something like pasta or pizza, chappatis are OK, but not every day. My Mum and Dad say ... once a week you will have Canadian food, otherwise "roti" all the time.' Almost all the students preferred to have sandwiches or another Canadian-style food for lunch during the school terms. As a Sikh girl commented: 'Curried vegetable would smell so much, so I don't bother'.

It is difficult to interpret mixed cooking. However, from our own experience of the communities and interviews, it became clear that mixed implied bought fish and chips, pies etc. or any other fast food. Very few families, though, actually cook English food at home. It is an increasing practice with a large number of Asian families to add on a little of the local popular food in their menus. For instance, breakfast consists mainly of toast and cereal and not 'paratha' and yoghurt as in the Punjab. Lunches are mostly taken at work places and may contain a mixture of food items from home and canteens. Overall, we would infer there is a change in food habits — another sign of acculturation.

## Language Spoken at Home

96% of the students are bilingual (at the spoken level) and a significant number (50%) can also read and write their home language. A large majority (97%) preferred to speak English most of the time. A response from a Sikh boy reflects the attitude of many youngsters: 'I speak Punjabi with my parents and English with my brothers and sisters. If my parents talk to me in Punjabi then I answer them in Punjabi — not every time though — sometimes in English.' To the question 'Are you learning Punjabi?' his response was 'Yes, at school not at the Gurudwara. My parents are pleased and I like it too'. There was no significant difference between the two groups.

Over 90% expressed the wish to learn their mother-tongue. From our observations we gathered that nearly all the Muslim boys and girls, except one, have actually done so at the mosque. 10% are not in favour of learning their mother-tongue; the common objection is on functional grounds. A Sikh girl commented: 'I am doing French and not Punjabi at school. I find it difficult to learn Punjabi anyway; I can pick up Punjabi at home — not French. This way I would have another language'. Some boys and girls were too embarrassed to speak in their mother-tongue. A Hindu girl remarked: 'I was trying my Punjabi — which I can't speak very well — my friend made me feel embarrassed by laughing at my pronunciation'. This is reinforced by the fact that, whenever I broke into Punjabi/Hindu/Urdu during the interview, I could easily see the embarrassed look on students' faces — some flushed, others fidgeted. The youngsters responded enthusiastically when asked for suggestions for the teaching of mother-tongue: 'should be an optional subject in schools', 'should be taught after school hours in schools', 'should be taught in Mosques/Gurudwaras/Hindu temples at the weekend'. In fact all these strategies are employed by the Asian parents. However, the attitude of the staff in the schools towards bilingualism was not very positive. The head of modern languages in one of the schools casually remarked: 'No, I can't speak Punjabi — what is the use? I can speak Spanish and French fluently!!' The head and majority of the staff (nearly all white) of another school were of the opinion that Asian pupils need more practice in English rather than Urdu/Punjabi if they wanted to do well in the school examinations. Such opinions were expressed in various forms by the staff in all schools. We came to the conclusion that the teaching of the community languages was generally considered to be irrelevant and not in the best interests of the Asian pupils. It is worth noting, however, that all the schools, perhaps reluctantly, made provision for 'majority' mother-tongue teaching — Punjabi and Urdu. It is also interesting to note that the National Curriculum does not recognise Asian languages as equivalent to the modern European languages. Such an official and legal position does undermine the status of community languages.

The Canadian situation is similar to the one discussed above. The majority of students speak a 'mixture' of Punjabi/English or Hindi/English at home; normally Punjabi/Hindi is spoken with parents and English with siblings and friends. It may be concluded that most youngsters are bilingual. Here we have an example of the responses. A Hindu boy: 'I speak a mixture of two languages — Hindi with parents — with friends English, my mum taught us and she says it is a part of our culture and you should know it'.

The majority (80%) were in favour of learning their home language at a spoken level. A Sikh boy's reply is typical: 'We should learn Punjabi — (where?) anywhere in schools or Gurudwara ... it comes back from our ancestors ... I felt weird when I was in Punjab because I could not speak it.' A Sikh girl: 'To speak should be enough — no need for the knowledge of reading and writing ... I have learnt it from parents'. This girl, regrettably it may be argued, articulates the opinion of the majority of youngsters we interviewed and others we met and talked to.

It is interesting to note, in this context, the state of language schools organised by Sikh communities in Vancouver, Surrey and Abbotsfield. Resources at these schools are quite inadequate to fulfil the function they profess to undertake. Poorly trained and paid teachers, outmoded books, unfamiliar material and illustrations, large classes and often uninteresting and dogmatic methods of teaching are regrettably features of these schools. They cannot possibly compete with the state-funded schools in their facilities. Thus, it is not surprising to find the poor attendance rate and high drop-out rate at Sunday schools. A similar situation is to be found in community schools in Birmingham.

Almost all the students, except four, have been to a Sunday school to learn Punjabi/Hindi. Their views and opinions of these schools are very often negative. A Sikh girl: 'I stopped going two years ago — I went there for six years ... I did not learn very much — I can't read very well ... (can you write?) — I can't write'.

## Religion

Though no significant difference was found between the two groups, it is clear from the Table 2.21 that the Muslim boys and girls are good attenders. A Muslim boy remarked: 'I have read the Koran two times — I fast on Ramadan and can also read Arabic and understand the meaning of the holy verses.' A Muslim girl responded: 'I have read the Koran in English. It says, for instance, you pray when you are sober ... meaning you might have been drinking!!!!' From the transcripts we inferred that Muslim boys and girls, for a variety of reasons, were more knowledgeable about their religion. In contrast, the Hindu and Sikh youngsters did not accord the same importance to their respective religions. Even the regular attenders did not show the same degree of commitment as their Muslim peers. A Sikh boy said: 'I go to the Gurudwara twice a week and also learn Punjabi. I know the names of the ten gurus and "Phali Pori", the first fundamental verse of Japji Sahib (the morning prayer of the Sikhs)'. A Sikh girl complained: 'I don't understand much at the Gurudwara — I look at my mother and do what she does and says. I can't say the prayer in Punjabi — but I pray in English.' Another Sikh girl commented: 'I am not a Pukka Sikh — I go to the Gurudwara on special occasions ... anyway you don't learn anything about the religion as everything is "old" Punjabi, and the "Bhai" (priest) does not speak English'.

It was commented upon repeatedly by the Hindu and Sikh students that they would like to know more about their respective religions, but as the ethos of the worshipping places is very archaic and traditional in form, style and presentation, it is virtually impossible for them to learn anything substantial — apart from the fact that they absorb the reverent atmosphere of the holy temples.

**Table 2.21** Attendance at Temples/Mosques — Birmingham sample

|                | Frequently | Sometimes | Never | Total |
|----------------|------------|-----------|-------|-------|
| Hindus & Sikhs | 10         | 13        | 7     | 30    |
| Muslims        | 11         | 8         | 1     | 20    |
| Total          | 21         | 21        | 8     | 50    |

It seems to us that Hindu and Sikh communities are far too lax/liberal on the issue of religious instruction. If they wish to impart knowledge of their respective religions, they have to seriously re-think the staffing of the Sunday schools and more importantly consider the appointment of English-speaking priests and provide books and other illustrative material in modern style, form and presentation.

The majority (18/25) of Indo-Canadian students attend their family's place of worship: nine go regularly and the rest on special occasions, such as weddings or on special religious ceremonies. But their knowledge of their religion is very rudimentary. Most of them have picked it up from their parents' informal chats and not from the Gurudwaras, contrary to expectation. We had a list of simple questions on the basic teachings and beliefs of Hindu and Sikh religions. None of the students, save two, could answer more than the first two questions, namely, knowledge of the founder and one or two basic principles. Here is a reply from a Sikh girl which sums up the situation: 'I know the "Mool Mantar", but I don't understand what's going on, I tried to listen in the Gurudwara — but I don't understand their "Old" Punjabi. No I have quit going — I guess I was not good enough.' Another girl commented: 'I really don't know what is going on — I know a teeny bit — ... I don't know the name of the founder ... (name of the holy book?) No.' A reply from a Hindu girl is also typical of the non-attenders: 'We have a temple at home — we pray to Ram and Sita — Lakshmi (Goddess of Wealth) and Hanuman (mythological popular monkey God) ... (Do you understand the significance of Diwali? — It is a festival of light, but I don't know why'.

The impression left on me after reading the interview transcripts was that these Indo-Canadian youngsters were keen to know about their religion, but that the priests (Bhai and Brahmin) in the Gurudwara and temples could neither speak English fluently nor could they express religious beliefs and doctrines in a relevant idiom, e.g. stories or anecdotes which could interest the youngsters. Consequently, the students have a very superficial knowledge of their religion, and most of them do not show the same degree of respect and reverence as their parents do. Of course, this is partly owing to the nature of the Canadian society in which these youngsters are growing up; it is secular in outlook.

The situation in both locales, therefore, is very similar indeed: the teaching of Hindu and Sikh religions is badly done. This is in sharp contrast to the Muslim groups in the UK and elsewhere. Muslim parents across the world are more particular about the teaching of their religion and this ties in with our findings.

## Friendship Patterns

Over 64% of the youngsters who responded to this question preferred to have friends from within their own respective ethnic group, though a significant number (32%) have friends from amongst the West Indians and whites. There was not even a single case mentioned of inter-gender friendship in the sample — showing the strong grip of home values on the youngsters.

**Table 2.22** Choice of friends — Birmingham sample

|                  | Mostly Asians | Mixed | Mostly white | No response |       |
| ---------------- | ------------- | ----- | ------------ | ----------- | ----- |
| Hindus & Sikhs   | 16            | 9     | 1            | 4           |       |
| Muslims          | 11            | 4     | 1            | 4           |       |
| Total            | 27            | 13    | 2            | 8           | =50   |

No significant differences between the groups.

As regards the main reason for not having white friends, it was commented upon again and again that 'there aren't that many whites in the school or in the street where we live'. Anyway, all Asian or black or white schools are in a very difficult position to foster inter-cultural understanding in a practical way. This is both an educational and an economic problem worthy of serious discussion.

As regards friendship patterns in the Vancouver sample, it was interesting to observe that there was a fair degree of cross-ethnic friendship, though not cross-gender in the case of Indo-Canadian. This was confirmed during the interview sessions. This is a sharp contrast to the situation in Birmingham.

The friendship choices were wide and varied. None of the students admitted to having friends exclusively from their own ethnic groups but, on further probing, two of them admitted to having intimate friends from within their own community. This cross-ethnic friendship pattern is very encouraging for the development of multicultural Vancouverian society. Here we have a selection of the responses: 'My best friend is Danny — he is a Fijian. Most of my friends go to other schools. I have mixed friends — East Indians, English/whites — one or two Chinese'. 'My friends are from all groups — white, Chinese and Filipinos … I enjoy their company. Could be any one — I could not care about or colour. Most of friends are whites — they are really nice people'.

The schools in Vancouver, according to the information provided by the schools in Birmingham have increasingly become mono-ethnic. For that matter, most inner-city schools in the UK are increasingly becoming Asian or black or white — a disturbing trend against the development of a multicultural society.

## Choice of Clothes and School Uniform

Nearly 83% of the Hindu and Sikh youths are allowed some say when parents buy clothes as compared to 45% of the Muslim families — a significant difference (P<0.05). Six Hindu and Sikh parents give full freedom to their daughters (these are of mixed marriages). As far as wearing of school uniform is concerned, none of the boys and girls encountered any difficulties. All schools allowed and tolerated Indian/Pakistan styles of uniform. However, all Muslim girls except two commented that their parents are strict and against the wearing of European-style clothes at home. 'I have to change to Salwar Kameez and no high heels or make-up at home', said a Muslim girl. We heard from a source that a number of Muslim girls keep make-up kits in the school lockers and are adept in changing from 'demure-looking Pakistani girls to self-confident, attractive Western girls'. Thus living in two worlds can place a heavy burden on these youngsters. Hindu and Sikh girls, however, have an easier time. A Sikh girl: 'My parents let me choose my clothes — going to Gurudwara — we have to wear Punjabi suits'. A Hindu girl: 'I can wear jeans at home — but when visiting I wear Salwar Kameez.'

The boys and girls of our Vancouver sample had a lot more freedom as compared to the Birmingham youngsters: all except two girls were given full choice in the matter of clothes, but even these two girls said that they have a real say in the matter and that their parents do not force their tastes on them.

Here we have a real and significant difference between the two samples. The Canadian youngsters are a lot more Westernised as was also demonstrated on the attitude scale. They were ambivalent on the item regarding wearing of traditional clothes. Here we see the attitude being put into practice at a behavioural level.

## Entertainment

72% of the sample do not see Asian films or videos and only 18%, mostly Hindus and Sikhs, watch frequently. This shows a trend away from the Asian cultural idiom. This result contrasts sharply with our previous research finding in which 65% of the sample were fond of watching. Comments were: 'They are boring — it is the same story with small changes'. Those who did watch them commented very frequently along the lines: 'My Mum/Dad likes it, so I also watch.' — this is their (Mum and Dad's) main entertainment. A Hindu boy: 'Yes, sometimes I do, my parents view them every weekend, they (films) are quite funny — really different'.

**Table 2.23** Asian film videos and music — Birmingham sample

|  | *Frequently* | *Sometimes* | *Never* | |
|---|---|---|---|---|
| Hindus & Sikhs (Boys & Girls) | 7 | 4 | 19 | |
| Muslims | 2 | 1 | 17 | |
| Total | 9 | 5 | 36 | =50 |

More Hindu and Sikh youngsters listen to 'Bhangra' music (Punjabi rock) than the Muslim young people (50% and 30% respectively — no significant difference, though). The main reason for this is that the popular Bhangra groups have been formed by youngsters whose parents emigrated from the 'Indian Punjab'. Therefore these groups have less appeal for the Muslim youths. There is another factor worth mentioning: the popular Pakistani music is more in the domain of religious/devotional (Kwalis) and, therefore, does not appeal to the younger generation. Overall, we note the shift away from Asian to modern pop music of the 'top thirty type' — reflecting another cultural shift. A Moslem girl: 'I listen to English music — don't like Indian — it is all the same. English songs make sense — they sing clearly'.

Here we have clear-cut evidence that the majority still likes to listen to Asian music and watch Indian films in the company of their parents. But all the respondents who say 'Yes' to Asian music also affirmed that they also listen to 'Rock' or 'funk' music. A significant number (10/25) also watch Asian programmes on the TV.

**Table 2.24** Asian music and videos — Canadian sample

|                | Yes | No |    |
| -------------- | --- | -- | -- |
| Asian Music    | 16  | 9  | 25 |
| Asian Videos   | 16  | 9  | 25 |

This pattern suggests a considerable attachment to the traditional forms of entertainment: however, this does not mean they do not enjoy English-medium films and music. Here we have another example of bicultural tastes amongst the youngsters similar to the ones we found in the case of food habits. Here is another area of difference between the two samples. This may relate to the fact that in Vancouver there is more scope on TV for ethnic programmes. One evening a week is devoted to Indian music, films and news of the community and this has proven to be very popular with the Asian Community.

## Arranged Marriages

This is a very sensitive topic for Asian boys and girls as most parents would prefer to continue with their traditional systems of arranged marriage. Therefore questions on this problematic issue were not asked until we felt sure that we had won the students' confidence and that we showed genuine interest in their welfare and were not just being 'nosey'. We did not discuss this issue with five boys and girls because it was felt that they might feel offended, but their responses are included in the no response category.

More Hindu and Sikh boys and girls as compared to the Muslims, are prepared to accept arranged marriage, though the majority of the whole sample are in doubt or ambivalent. A Muslim boy encapsulates this feeling: 'I don't know yet — it is a long way away.' Another Muslim boy remarked: 'My Dad's wish is that it (marriage) should be within our relatives — on Mum's side. I don't mind if she is an educated girl, nice and from a good family.' A Sikh boy supported the arranged marriage: 'I think I would like an arranged marriage — but I would like to meet my would-be fiancée a couple of times before the ceremony.' Those who opposed argued for individual/personal choice. A Sikh boy: 'No, I won't accept it, I will marry at 22. I got to have a choice'. Muslim girl: 'My sister is marrying her boyfriend — lucky sod! I have told my uncle (she lives with his family) I will not accept it'.

**Table 2.25** Arranged marriages — Birmingham sample

|                   |       | *Accept* | *No* | *Don't Know* |
|-------------------|-------|----------|------|--------------|
| Hindus & Sikhs    | Boys  | 3        | 1    | 9            |
|                   | Girls | 7        | 1    | 8            |
| Muslims           | Boys  | 2        | 1    | 6            |
|                   | Girls | 1        | 2    | 9            |
| Total             |       | 13       | 5    | 32  =50      |

More Hindu and Sikh youngsters are willing to accept arranged marriage. This may be partly due to the fact that the Indian community is slightly more liberal and is willing to modify the arranged marriage custom: girls and boys are allowed to meet in a family situation before the betrothal ceremony, allowing a degree of choice, and there is no insistence that marriage partners should be from back home. A similar picture emerged from the boys and girls in Vancouver: 13 boys and girls did not respond to this question, two agreed with the practice, five were not sure and the remaining five (four girls and one boy) were against this custom.

Here is a reply from a Sikh girl who shows a degree of adjustment to the Canadian way of life. 'My dad wants to marry me fast — so he can have a bigger family (her mother died a year ago) ... but I want to be a pharmacist — takes four years — he wants the worry off his shoulders — he is 54: then he says it is up to you — I will support, if you want to go to a University.' Another Sikh girl commented: 'It is good in some way ... I would get choice ... I want somebody in Canada (anyone?) — no not outside the community.'

A Hindu girl replied: 'My brother and sister had arranged marriages, so there is no doubt I will get it too!, but I got to know this person really well before I say "Yes". If I don't like him, I have to say "No" ... boy is likely to be from India'. This girl articulated the feelings of most youngsters: they do not want to go against their parents' wishes, but would like some say and choice in the matter. But the majority of youngsters settle for a 'form' of arranged marriage. According to my deep knowledge of Asian communities, both in Canada and Britain, a modified form of arranged marriage has replaced the orthodox practice where bride and bridegroom met for the first time on their wedding night. A response from a Sikh girl is illuminating: 'it is changing a little. People will get to know before marriage ... as long as children are good and parents trust them, they would give more choice ... my mum says as long as you behave responsibly'. It appears that a middle way is being followed by most parents. Most marriages are arranged with the consent of youngsters and partners are also chosen from within the communities settled in Britain, Canada and the USA.

The related issue of dating was not probed owing to the perceived sensitivity of parents on this issue. It would have been quite inappropriate for me to violate the trust which the parents placed in me by agreeing to have their daughter/son interviewed. But my intuition and inside knowledge of the Indo-Community, tells me that this is, and is likely to continue to be, a growing area of difficulty between the two generations. Furthermore, as boys are allowed more freedom generally, girls are increasingly going to resent it, and perhaps some would revolt over the marriage issue. It is, after all, the girls who have to accept the traditional role of a wife, with its concomitant obligations of running a home, rearing kids and looking after the elderly, whereas men usually enjoy independence and dominance over their wives in the traditional family set-up. However, there is some evidence (mainly personal observation of the community) that the traditional norms are changing somewhat, especially in the middle classes, and men are more willing to help out in running the family life.

## Equality of Treatment

78% of the sample think that girls are treated differently, boys getting favourable treatment in all aspects of living. A Muslim girl reported: 'No, not at all, it is a man's world. Men are on top of everything. The way they do it is very discreet. In our own system, they openly say so and women have to accept it'. A Muslim boy: 'No, my sisters stay at home — this is our tradition'. Muslim girls expressed their views very strongly about the injustices they have to suffer. Here is a comment from a very attractive Muslim girl: 'My brother plays till 8 — he is allowed out. I go home, do my homework, watch TV and sleep. It is like a rota. Next day is exactly the same — weekends are the same.' Hindu girls were less resentful: 'No, but I don't think boys and girls should go against their parents' will. They should do what they say. I would make sure that boys do more than what they do now.' A Hindu boy: 'My sister gets the same treatment —

same freedom — she can go and see her friends — as I can (second thoughts) — just about.' It may be that the Hindus and Sikhs' parents are less strict than the Muslims. A Muslim girl: ' ... men are all force and women are stuck in the house. Boys can go out with any girls they want to — parents don't say anything — but if they find out girls are doing it — they go crazy, it is so stupid — it is not fair. Hindus and Sikhs give more freedom, Muslims are very strict about their daughters.'

**Table 2.26** Equal treatment of boys and girls — Birmingham sample

|                  | Yes | No | No response |      |
| ---------------- | --- | -- | ----------- | ---- |
| Hindus & Sikhs   | 5   | 20 | 5           |      |
| Muslims          | 0   | 18 | 2           |      |
| Total            | 5   | 38 | 7           | =50  |

Differences are not significant between the groups.

In the Vancouver sample a slightly higher proportion, nearly half, of boys and girls think they are treated the same. However, I am sceptical of their responses. Perhaps there was a tendency to give me the 'desired' response. According to their teachers and counsellors (their opinion to be discussed in Chapter 3), differential treatment of boys and girls at home gives rise to a lot of resentment in girls. Girls are not allowed to participate in games and other school activities, whereas boys are encouraged to do so, particularly in sports. However, here are some of the responses. A Sikh boy: 'Not really ... most parents are old fashioned, but depends'. A Hindu boy: 'No equality ... my sister helps already I won't do it, it's girls' job to work in the kitchen'. A Hindu girl: 'Boys are better treated ... well the main thing is not able to go out with your friends ... I like to go. They think in early teens daughters should be protected'. Another Hindu girl: 'No, I live under curfew — I have to be in by 6.00, but I can handle it, you have to be smart'.

The notion of curfew was very intriguing to me, so I sought an explanation from the teachers. It was explained that Indo-Canadian parents are not willing for their daughters to go out after school, especially in winter months. Boys are often allowed this freedom, and parents even turn a blind eye if they date white girls — which they often do. Girls perceive this treatment to be utterly unfair and complain bitterly to their counsellors.

It seems to be that Hindu and Sikh parents are increasingly giving more educational opportunities to their daughters, but still are more protective in the social sphere. For instance, most parents would like their daughters to pursue higher education, but in the home area where they can keep an eye on their personal and social life. This situation is bound to change when the present second-generation girls bring up their sons and daughters.

Drury (1991) reports similar findings from her research on Sikh girls in Nottingham. 66% said they do not support arranged marriages; however the majority will accept it. The majority resented the fact that boys are given the freedom to go out and even date white girls, when they are also supposed to accept arranged marriages.

## Favourite Subjects and Vocational Aspirations

Choice of favourite subjects was very mixed indeed, though boys tended to go for maths and science whereas girls chose arts. There were 16 students who did not volunteer any information on this topic. A Muslim girl: 'I enjoy them all really.' A Hindu boy: 'I haven't thought about it.' To the question 'which one do you enjoy most?': 'all of them' was the prompt response. There were no group differences.

The favourite subject amongst the boys in Vancouver is physical education (7/13), and as for the rest of the subjects, the opinions are fairly evenly distributed. Amongst the girls they are once again evenly spread.

**Table 2.27** Vocational aspirations — Birmingham sample

|                  | Professional | Non-Professional | Don't Know |     |
| ---------------- | ------------ | ---------------- | ---------- | --- |
| Hindus & Sikhs   | 15           | 7                | 8          |     |
| Muslims          | 4            | 5                | 11         |     |
| Total            | 19           | 12               | 19         | =50 |

Difference between the two groups is significant. Further analysis showed that, whereas eight Hindu and Sikh girls want to enter professions, only two Muslim girls showed aspiration in that direction. A Muslim girl lamented: 'My parents won't let me go to college to study to become air hostess. They think education for girls is useless'. A Sikh girl, on the contrary, asserted confidently: 'I want to be a doctor — I have taken the right course for that'. To the question 'would your parents let you?', the response was very affirmative: 'They encouraged me.'

**Table 2.28** Vocational aspirations — Vancouver sample

|        | *Professional* | *Non-professional* | *Don't Know* |      |
|--------|:---:|:---:|:---:|:---:|
| Boys   | 3  | 6  | 4  |      |
| Girls  | 8  | 4  | –  |      |
| Total  | 11 | 10 | 4  | =25  |

It is interesting to note, that despite the expressed unequal treatment, most of the girls cherish ambitions to enter professional careers. It may be inferred that Indo-Canadian parents are, perhaps, strict with regard to dating and seeing them going out alone or with friends for shopping or for meals, but as far as education is concerned they are willing for their girls to go to college and the like to realise their aspirations. Regrettably some teachers tend to generalise, and even stereotype, that all Asian girls are discouraged by parents from entering higher education and pursuing professional careers.

**Table 2.29** Attend college — Birmingham sample

|                  | *Yes* | *No* | *Don't Know* |      |
|------------------|:---:|:---:|:---:|:---:|
| Hindus & Sikhs   | 18 | 9  | 3  |      |
| Muslims          | 12 | 7  | 1  |      |
| Total            | 30 | 16 | 4  | =50  |

60% of the sample intend to go to college for further education and 32% would leave school to enter work. Five Muslims and nine Hindu and Sikh girls had intentions to go to college. Whether these would be realised is another matter.

In the Vancouver sample, all the youngsters, except one, intended to stay on in school for graduation which is at 18, and (18/25), a high proportion, would like to go to college and the like for further education and training.

In both schools, over 80% Indo-Canadian, and indeed other ethnic group students, stay on until 18, according to the principals of the schools. This is markedly higher than the statistics for the Birmingham schools, where only around 60% of the students stay on for 'A' levels and other examinations.

## Asian Teachers

The above-listed responses were to the question: 'Do you think there should be more Asian teachers?' This was quite a surprising finding in that Asian parents (Ghuman, 1980) and educationalists (Verma, 1986; Swann, 1985) generally are of the view that the presence of Asian teachers is desirable for a variety of sound reasons. But here we have 38% against the 44% in the don't know or have no opinion category. A perceptive Muslim girl comments: 'There ought to be more Asian teachers in white schools and vice versa — so you can mix. English and Asian should mix — if you stick Asians together and whites together nothing would ever change'.

**Table 2.30** Asian teachers — Birmingham sample

|                | Yes | No | Don't Know |       |
| -------------- | --- | -- | ---------- | ----- |
| Hindus & Sikhs | 5   | 11 | 14         |       |
| Muslims        | 4   | 8  | 8          |       |
| Total          | 9   | 19 | 22         | =50   |

I think it is interesting to quote a response, at some length, of a Hindu girl from Delhi who was here for four years: 'I would choose a school like this (rather than one I went to in India)'. Why? 'Freedom: you can talk to teachers and it is a good thing if you want to make progress in our studies — I be missing this school, but not this country! Here you are free to make choices — teachers listen to you — less punishment and we don't get any homework (*sic*) — only in some subjects. If you look at the Indian girls here, they don't have freedom at all. They are not allowed to cut hair, wear suits, their parents are really strict. But, even though I live in India, I am allowed to cut my hair, wear what I like. English girls have freedom, but not Indian girls'. Finally an indictment on the

Indian system: 'In India teaehers have the right to hit you — not here. And a lot of homework (in India) and discipline is much better in India'. Of course this girl comes from the urban upper-middle class in India.

A Sikh boy had a sound reason for not having Asian teachers: 'No, it is a good thing really (that there aren't any) — because kids swear a lot in Punjabi and teachers would know it and might tell our parents'. Another Sikh girl had a similar reply: 'I can confide in white teachers, but I daren't do with Asians — they might tell my parents'. Other responses:

A Hindu boy: 'Yes, as long as they can teach — I don't mind.'

A Sikh boy: 'Yes, they would help with the language problem'.

A Hindu boy: 'It depends — quite a few in here (3/35) should be a "mix" variety — few more black teachers we need.'

My impression was that the majority did not care either way as they were generally satisfied with the teachers. But a dissatisfied Sikh boy commented cynically: 'I am not happy — teachers leave quickly. We had four teachers in maths, four in physics in last two terms'.

In the Canadian sample, interestingly, 13 say 'Yes' and 12 respond 'doesn't matter'. The typical replies were: 'It is a good idea, just like other teachers — it gives our people a chance'; 'Yes, I love it — you feel proud'.

However, it is difficult to interpret the difference between the British and the Canadian sample. The British boys and girls were against the idea. It may be that in Vancouver schools there were only two teachers belonging to ethnic minorities, whereas in three Birmingham schools there were six class teachers in addition to two senior teachers — a deputy head and a head.

## Racial Prejudice

The overwhelming majority (96%) of the sample agreed that there is racism in this country, and a majority (84%) said they have had personal experience of it. A Sikh boy remarked: 'Yes, I have been called names, Pakis — I get upset, I sometimes would like to beat them up or call them names back. Sometimes I tell my Dad; teachers sometimes tell them off or say go and fight back'. Another Sikh boy: 'Yes, a lot of time, it was every day — but it is better now. I do react to them. Yesterday a black kid called me a Paki — I called him a nigger. Indians are also racist to whites and even to fellow Indians in this area — therefore whites want to get out — they are in minority'. A mixed parentage Muslim girl: 'Yes, there is a lot of prejudice — not against me, but I have seen it and racial abuse. It is not bad around. I meet people from both sides. My mum's dad (white man) didn't like my father — he is a bit racist. But he is getting on'.

**Table 2.31** Racial prejudice — Birmingham sample

|                   | Yes | Don't Know | No  |     |
| ----------------- | --- | ---------- | --- | --- |
| Hindus & Sikhs    | 25  | 1          | 2   |     |
| Muslims           | 18  | 2          | 2   |     |
| Total             | 43  | 3          | 4   | =50 |

None of the boys and girls from Vancouver admitted to having met any overt racial prejudice — which is remarkable. It is very hard to say how far they were being truthful. But they seemed to be most confident in their answers and felt secure in their Indo-Canadian identity — a point which I shall discuss subsequently.

## Equality of Opportunity

The results are similar to the question on racism. The majority believe they will not get equal treatment. A Muslim boy: 'I want to get a job on equal basis'. Would it upset you if you didn't? 'Yes — but my brother has a shop so I might work in the family business'. A number of youngsters echoed this sentiment. A Sikh girl reasoned: 'Well in a way sometimes they are right — when they say bad things — my cousins come and park everywhere. The (neighbours) phone the police about the noise should understand our tradition — but they are ... (pause) wrong, when they blame Indian people for everything — like the Indian people are taking over all the shops'. This girl, like many other youngsters, was desperately trying to be fair and objective on this emotive issue, and trying to understand the feeling of the prejudiced whites. A Muslim girl argued: 'I don't think they hate you or the colour — it is just that they think you are different and you are not supposed to be here. Why should be here? Go back to your country — they shout. Cos, little they think you are also poor and you live in a council flat ... they are sort of frightened.' A somewhat confused comment, but she wanted to get at the root of the problem. A number of youngsters, without prompting, expressed the view that their school is free from racism — an encouraging sign of inter-cultural harmony. A Sikh boy (with turban): 'Teachers are quite fair — no prejudice here.' A Hindu boy: 'Teachers are very nice — understanding. Like normal people, kind.'

**Table 2.32** Equality of opportunity in jobs — Birmingham sample

|  | Yes | No | Don't Know |  |
| --- | --- | --- | --- | --- |
| Hindus & Sikhs | 1 | 25 | 4 |  |
| Muslims | 1 | 18 | 1 |  |
| Total | 2 | 43 | 5 | =50 |

A Muslim girl remarked: 'I won't get a job same as a white girl. My chances are 20% less because of my colour. I would not give up — try again and again … it is not your loss — it is their loss because you are better qualified. Also it is up to us to improve'. On racism the same girl remarked: 'My parents are very racist against this black girl (a girl she is friendly with in school). They shout at me saying don't hang about with a girl like her.' But a Muslim boy believed he would get a fair chance. His reasoning was: 'Yes, I think it is fair in this country — our people should try harder. When I qualify I think I shall get a fair chance'. A Hindu girl expressed a similar sentiment: 'I am treated fairly — I treat them (whites) fairly as well. Some English people think we are going to take over … it frightens them'.

My impression is that most of the youngsters are quite realistic about their employment opportunity in a white-dominated market, but are prepared to study further to gain higher qualifications to counteract the effect of racial discrimination. Some have worked out alternative strategies. They would work in a family business or start their own business; some said they might emigrate to Canada.

**Table 2.33.** Equality of opportunity — Vancouver sample

|  | Yes | No | Not sure/Don't Know |  |
| --- | --- | --- | --- | --- |
| Boys | 13 | 0 | 1 | =14 |
| Girls | 10 | 0 | 1 | =11 |
| Total | 23 | 0 | 2 | 25 |

Thus the overwhelming majority think they would be 'equally' treated in the job market. This is a surprising finding; in the Birmingham sample it is quite the reverse — the vast majority think they would be discriminated against. Their answers are revealing. A Sikh girl replies: 'Yes, I think I will — in a job all they want is education, if you have it — you be OK.' A Hindu boy commented 'I hope so, (you are not sure?) ... some people think differently, they don't like East Indians. Some are racist. Maybe 1 out of 10 would be of this type. I haven't met any racism ... my uncle is owner of a dentist shop, he started from the bottom and made it.'

My impression after the interview was that these youngsters shared the North American dream of their parents: 'to get to the top all you need is hard work and the right qualifications'. This is in sharp contrast to the perceptions of young British Asians who believe you ought to have at least 'twice' the qualifications of whites to stand a chance.

## Identity

The question on ethnic identity was: 'Do you feel English/British or British/Hindu or Indian/Pakistani?'.

The majority felt they are British/Sikhs etc. rather than English or Indian or Pakistani. It is interesting to note that the identity of the youngsters is tied to their religion rather than to their parents' original nationalities. A Sikh boy commented: 'I can't say I am English — they will laugh at me. I think I am a British/Sikh in a way'. Almost all the youngsters repeated such comments with variations. However, those who thought they were English/British commented along the following lines: 'I was born in England — so I am English or British. My religion is a different matter.'

**Table 2.34** Ethnic identity — Birmingham sample

|  | Don't Know | English/ British | British/Muslim/Hindu Identity | Asian |  |
|---|---|---|---|---|---|
| Hindu & Sikh | 3 | 3 | 23 | 1 |  |
| Muslim | 2 | 1 | 15 | 2 |  |
| Total | 5 | 4 | 38 | 3 | =50 |

The interviews left the impression that the majority of the youngsters would, in fact, feel and be treated as strangers if they were to move to the country of their parents' origin. Despite the widespread racial discrimination and unemployment in the community, they felt Britain to be their home country.

The picture in Vancouver, however, is very different. To the question: 'Do you feel Canadian or East Indian, or Indo-Canadian?' — the overwhelming reply was 'Indo-Canadian' (20/25); a small number also opting for just Canadian (5). No one responded 'a Sikh' or 'a Hindu' or 'an East Indian', to my surprise. The youngsters' self-confidence and positive self-image was remarkable. A reply like the following was common: 'I feel Canadian, I guess so — (pause) I am Indo-Canadian.' A Hindu/Christian girl's response shows a desire to change and adapt (do you feel Canadian or Indo-Canadian?): 'I don't know — I follow other religion — I try to go to Church, I try to fit; I do my best — I still believe in my religion (i.e. Hindu), but I can fit in both religions (pause) you have to — I do. I was raised here, I was a baby; my parents tried to make me Hindi *(sic)* — but I mixed with East Indians and white people. They (parents) have accepted my biculturalism'.

It is indeed encouraging to note that the official Canadian policy of multiculturalism is having an effect on our Indo-Canadian youngsters; they are almost proud of their bicultural identities and feel secure and feel that Canada is their home country.

## Parents' Country

54% have been back (mostly on holiday) to their parents' country of origin and thoroughly enjoyed themselves. A Sikh girl: 'I went to India — yes it is brilliant. Shanker village house was nice, I made some friends there.' A Muslim boy: 'I have been back three times, it is a nice country — it is open, there are fields and horses ... it is too hot'. Those who have not been longing to go. A Muslim girl: 'No I haven't been back, I like to go — my relatives' place. I wouldn't like to live there.' This was the sentiment of the majority of the youngsters. But a few were quite unequivocal in saying no. A Muslim girl: 'No, I wouldn't like to go'. Why? 'You won't get that much freedom — it is too hot'. Another Muslim girl: 'I went to Pakistan when I was very young — no, not now — people who are close to me had bad experiences — forced to get married, he was 17 at that time.' Only a couple of boys said they would like to go back to live. A Hindu boy said: 'I have been to Punjab twice — it is a nice place to go. I want to go back and live there.' A Muslim boy: 'Yes, I lived in Pakistan for 5 years, though I was born here. I would like to go back

— to open farms and animals. People are nice and real friendly there.' The majority expressed the view that they would like to go back to visit, but not to stay permanently. Further, most of them said they enjoyed living in this country despite the problems facing their family. A Hindu girl: 'I like the English people — on the whole I like living in this country.' A Sikh boy: 'I like living in H..., I like my school — separate' (means single-sex).The youngsters of the Vancouver sample feel the same way. 16 students have been back to India/Fiji to see their parents' indigenous villages and towns. All of them enjoyed their visits, but none wanted to go and live there; but they would go again for holidays or to attend wedding ceremonies.

**Table 2.35** Visited parents' country of origin — Birmingham sample

|                  | Yes | No |     |
| ---------------- | --- | -- | --- |
| Hindus & Sikhs   | 15  | 15 |     |
| Muslims          | 12  | 8  |     |
| Total            | 27  | 23 | =50 |

Here are a few sample replies: 'My (pind) village is near Jallundar — we lived in Basipur, my dad's brother live there. All our relatives live close to you. I saw cows, a dairy farm. But Vancouver is very clean.

'Yes I have been back, I like beaches — it is like tropical — my grandma and grandpa live there.'

For these youngsters, Vancouver is home now; sentimental attachment to the country of origin is a passing first-generation phenomenon.

## General Discussion

Attitudes are defined as 'a more or less stable set or disposition of opinion ... and readiness with an appropriate response' (Drever, 1962: 22). The acculturation scale measures culture change. Opinions held by an individual do influence her/his behaviour, but do not necessarily determine it. But through my long interviews with the youngsters I was able to assess their behaviour, as well as their opinions, on important personal, social and cultural aspects of living. The response patterns elicited by both assessment techniques converged to a remarkable degree. There are four main inferences which we can draw from our scale and interview data.

First, the youngsters wish to retain the core values of their home culture: namely language, Asian names, aspects of religion and family cohesion. Mary Stopes-Roe & Cochrane (1990) also report research findings along the same lines. Drury (1991), in her study with a sample of Sikh girls in Nottingham, found that a large majority wants the teaching of Punjabi to be a part of the primary school curriculum and that schools should also have a qualified Sikh Priest (Granthe) to instruct children in their religion, where there is a viable number of children to benefit from such arrangements.

Most Asian names are derived from the holy religious texts and have significant symbolic and emotional meanings for the individuals. Some teachers, by constant mispronunciation of Asian names, put sub-conscious pressure on students to Anglicise their names or to adopt a British/Canadian name. We have come across very many examples where teachers overtly criticise names as 'foreign' (even ridicule them) and sometimes give English names to children. Of course, there may be some instances where an Asian name can be a matter of ridicule or abuse, such as Nashitar Kaur, which was cruelly abbreviated to Shit Kaur. In these cases teachers can advise parents and students to alter 'ambiguous or embarrassing' names to more socially acceptable ones.

Secondly, most youngsters support the idea of mixing with indigenous whites. They reject the 'ghetto mentality' of sticking to their own respective ethnic group. But, a lot depends upon the attitudes of the indigenous white group (the dominant group — which in both countries is Celtic/Anglo-Saxon). If the majority opinions are racist and these are expressed both covertly and overtly, then the minority ethnic groups might (and do) revert to the security of their own enclave. These enclaves are to be found in Britain as well as in Canada. Chinatowns are well established all over North America (Vancouver has the second largest) and in Manchester and London (UK). So is 'little Punjab' in Southall and Handsworth by the Sikh communities.

Thirdly, the youngsters reject, or are ambivalent about, some of the customs of their families, the most troublesome being the tradition of arranged marriages. Drury (1991) also found this amongst Sikh girls in Nottingham: the majority of girls rejected this custom (65%), but also were resigned to accepting it in the long run. Most Asian parents are making changes, but they probably are not radical enough for the youngsters. I shall take up this theme again in Chapter 4.

Fourthly, most Asian girls in our sample feel they are not treated on a par with the boys. Asian parents are more protective towards their daughters and also consider it a question of Izzat (honour) that their girls should not be seen in pubs, or going out and loitering, especially in the company of boys. Some parents are very strict and deny further education and/or career opportunities to their daughters. There are no easy solutions to this problem, but better communication between the home and school should help the situation. Likewise, the employment of ethnic counsellors would be a move in the right direction.

There is an interesting case of an Indian Muslim girl which illustrates this dilemma. During her university years this girl took to drinking, smoking and dating white boys ... the so-called 'bad ways of the whites' in her parents' eyes. Her family was naturally very angry about her behaviour and give her the ultimatum: 'Give up the evil ways and return to the family fold or you are on your own.' In the event, she decided to go her own way. During her teacher-training course she became quite ill and needed the support of her boyfriend. But her boyfriend left her for some reason. She felt devastated as she had nobody to turn to for help in her moment of crisis. She began regretting her decision to abandon her family and kinship group. After a number of counselling sessions with me, she decided to approach her family with a view to 'repent' and to ask to be taken back. She was fortunate in that her parents were understanding and agreed to support her in every way, provided she would not follow the same path again. There are other cases where such transgressions would have led to a permanent split; and some transgressions are threatened with severe punishment to square the family's Izzat.

Finally, it became quite clear that the Canadian students are far more positively inclined to accept the norms and values of the society. They seemed to be more confident and sure of their claims to be Indo-Canadian, with full rights and responsibilities. The political climate in Canada has changed since the 1970s. Politicians of all persuasions (from the federal ministers down to provincial governments) have been in favour of pluralism. There was a black policy co-ordinating minister for multicultural education in 1988. The Vancouver Schools Board (1989) has a clear policy statement on multicultural education and there is a co-ordinating officer to encourage, support and monitor the progress of schools towards cultural pluralism.

In Britain, however, the policy on multicultural education has changed since the introduction of the National Curriculum in 1988. It is to be treated as a cross-curricular theme, and in some cases the national subject committees recommend certain aspects of multicultural education to be incorporated into the teaching of a given subject. Some academics feel that multicultural education has been marginalised by the government policies (Troyna, 1990; Tomlinson, 1991).

There are also discordant opinions to be heard on the issues within multicultural education in Vancouver. The principal of a Sikh public school felt that: 'The religious and moral education is best catered for in a separate school. For the Sikh children to have high self-esteem and positive self-identify requires the teaching of Punjabi language and literature and "shabat kirtan" (devotional singing). High positive self-esteem is important for the Sikh youngsters to live honourably in a white-dominated Christian/secular society. Sikh children do pick up the customs and habits of the indigenous Canadians which often prove to be the major impediments to the perpetuation of Sikh religion and culture.' My request for research with youngsters was turned down on the grounds that the research techniques (attitude scale and interview) are 'learning experiences' *per se* and might upset the impressionable young minds. Similar views are held by some Muslims and Maulvis in the UK (Ashraf, 1988). A related fact is that denominational and public schools, both in the UK and Canada, have virtually no policies on multicultural education. Whether these incongruous voices are a threat to cultural pluralism and tolerance, or else precursors of true cultural diversity as they claim, only time will tell.

## Notes

1. The Birmingham data were further analysed by the method of Principal Component Analysis, using the SSP programme. A meaningful factor structure emerged from the analysis. The interested reader is referred to my paper which contains this information (Ghuman, 1991a: 121–32).
2. Likewise the Canadian data were analysed by the same method. Once again, a clear factor structure emerged. The results are reported in a paper to be published in the *International Journal of Adolescents and Youth*, March 1994.

# 3 Teachers' Opinions of Asian Adolescents

> I say look I have grown up in this environment, I had to fight battles … you must respect your parents' wishes. We have some girls who got up in conflict, they seem to struggle the most, especially Muslim girls. White teachers tend to over sympathise.… A Muslim parent came to school. He said: What is my daughter doing? So I took him around. He said: You are one of us, so you understand. Although I am very forth right, but I am very traditionist at heart. I can fit into both cultures. In Indian society, I behave like an Indian, here I behave like an English. I am bicultural. (Asian Woman Teacher)

It was considered important to ascertain the opinions and views of teachers on issues and concerns which have a bearing on students' bicultural identities. Next to parents and peers, teachers are probably the most influential people in students' lives. In the case of young people of Asian origin, it may be even more significant since for most of them it is their first protracted contact with white people both in Vancouver and Birmingham. The main reason for this is that a large majority of students live in exclusively ethnic areas (sometimes referred to as ghettos with negative connotations) with minimum contact with the indigenous white population. Students' perceptions of, and attitudes towards, indigenous whites are therefore largely derived from their contact with teachers as well as from the media.

## Samples

### Birmingham

I approached several members of the teaching staff, 18 in all for interview from the three chosen schools. Twelve teachers agreed and were happy to be interviewed, but only six agreed to be tape-recorded. To achieve a viable sample, another 15 teachers from other Birmingham schools were interviewed. These teachers are known to me through professional and personal contacts. Details of the sample are given in Table 3.1.

**Table 3.1** Teachers' sample from Birmingham

|                | Female |  | Male |      |
| -------------- | ------ | --- | ---- | ---- |
| Asians         | 5      |  | 10   | =15  |
| Afro-Caribbean | 1      |  | 3    | =4   |
| Whites         | 4      |  | 4    | =8   |
| Total          | 10     |  | 17   | =27  |

In addition, one home–school liaison teacher (male) and two social workers, both women, were included in the sample to obtain a wider picture of the concerns and anxieties of young people. Also the views of two Asian lecturers in Multicultural Education were obtained to supplement our data.

### Vancouver

The sample size from Vancouver is comparatively small; only 14 persons took part in the research. Of the teachers and school counsellors, eight are female and four male; three belong to ethnic minorities. Two home–school link workers (not teachers as is the case in Birmingham schools), both Punjabi women in their mid-careers, took part in the research. All, except one, had attended courses on multicultural education and a number (6) had good inside knowledge of the Indo-Canadian community through friends and professional contacts.

## Methodology

The technique of semi-structured interviewing has been used throughout our research endeavours to collect information from the respondents. Most teachers agreed to the use of a tape recorder, but a number (6/27) refused for a variety of reasons. In these cases, detailed notes were taken during the interview and impressions were added after the interview. A list of items on which semi-structured interviews were based is to be found in Appendix 6.

## Discussion

All three schools in Birmingham have resolved problems relating to the wearing of school uniform, school meals and mixed classes in physical education,

by judicious compromises between the strict demands of established school con-
ventions and the requirements of the home. A white, male history teacher
explained:

> ... one parent refused to allow his son to change in front of other boys —
> he says it is against the Koran. So the PE teacher made concessions on this
> point — likewise other problems have been resolved. To convince parents
> of the value of PE, Mr. S. quoted Koran to say ... you must benefit.
> Swimming and PE is separate for girls. Parents who won't allow their girls
> swimming ... their wishes are respected. Girls can wear salwar Kameez of
> the right colour and a head scarf if they so wish. School meals include veg-
> etable dishes ... most love chips anyway. Also halal meat is served.

Schools in Vancouver do not encounter any problems on these counts as there
is no compulsory uniform, and no provision is made for school meals. As regards
mixed classes for PE, the schools have made separate arrangements for girls.

## Bilingualism and the Teaching of Community Languages

Language is an important part of culture. It codifies, expresses and perpetu-
ates the myths, legends and sentiments of a society. Some scholars (Whorf,
1956) believe that it shapes our world views. He wrote:

> We dissect nature along lines laid by our native language. The categories and
> types that we isolate from the world of phenomena we do not find because
> they stare every observer in the face; on the contrary, the world is presented in
> a kaleidoscopic flux of impressions which has to be organized by our minds.
> We cut nature up, organize into concepts, and ascribe significance as we do
> largely because we are party to an agreement to organize it in this way ....
> (Whorf, 1956: 28).

Even if the so-called stronger version of the Whorfian hypothesis is unac-
ceptable, namely that language influences and shapes our world views, it is
undeniable that language plays an important role in the formation of our personal and social identities. This is particularly the case with ethnic minority
communities as their languages are closely linked to their religious texts, ritu-
als and practices.

### Birmingham

All the teachers in the Birmingham sample supported bilingualism and the
learning of the mother-tongue. But wide differences arose as to whether the

teaching should be part of the school curriculum. Over 3/4 (or 21) of the teachers believed that the teaching of community languages should be part of the school's function; otherwise community languages would lose status *both in the eyes of the pupils and teachers, and would come to be accepted as second rate.*

A male Asian teacher summarises the arguments:

> It is every child's birth right to learn his language — all schools should make adequate arrangements to do so ... the practical difficulties are often given as an excuse not to meet the first demands of ethnic communities. Even in the schools where it is implemented — poor facilities exist. Kids are often taught in cubby holes, with poor resources and sometimes by unqualified part-time teachers.

A teacher of Punjabi (Asian, male) was candid in his remarks:

> White teachers, generally speaking, regard it as second rate. (What way?) In various ways this comes up — we haven't got a slot in the school time; teaching during the dinner time. Then there is a question of rooms; any broom-cupboard will do. A lot depends on the teacher's standing in the school. If they respect you as a teacher not of Hindu/Punjabi only, then attitude is different ... i.e. it is better.

As described earlier, all three schools in our research do provide facilities for the teaching of 'majority' spoken languages. The schools have employed ethnic teachers to do this. However, the teachers who disagreed with the teaching of community languages in school time argued that it should be the responsibility of the parents and the community. A woman Asian TESL teacher argued:

> Personally, I feel it's parents' obligation to speak, make an effort to teach their kids. You have to make a decision in a school where there are six languages ... what I am saying is, its place is generally in the home. Anyway Section 11 funding would now support only the teaching of English.

Some suggested, (8/27) implicitly, that in terms of educational priorities it may not be a judicious choice. A white (male) headmaster commented:

> What these kids need is more practice in English and not in Urdu. They ought to speak English at home, listen to the radio and read English books. This is the only way they can achieve high academic standards. They might have a reasonable command of the spoken English, but they need to work at their written English ... though we do have classes in two community languages at school.

It is widely believed by Asian teachers (Ghuman, 1992) and Asian academics that most white teachers, especially the older age group (45+), do not really approve of Asian childrens' bilingualism. Furthermore, it is argued by some academics (Verma, 1986) that they still, mistakenly, believe in the assimilation policies of the early 1960s rather than the pluralistic approach suggested by the Swann Committee. Though the Swann report (1985) rejected the suggestion that the mother-tongue maintenance programmes, i.e. the development of pupils' mother-tongue fluency, should be an integral part of the primary school curriculum, it recommended the teaching of community languages as part of the secondary school modern languages curriculum. The committee also recommended that language diversity should be seen as a positive opportunity to broaden the horizons of all pupils.

### Vancouver

All teachers and counsellors supported bilingualism, i.e. learning of French and English. In addition all agreed with the view that students should learn their home language. A counsellor commented:

> Absolutely necessary — it would be better if languages were available as part of the curriculum, otherwise after school or weekend facilities should be, and are provided. On heritage language programme the school board supports these initiatives — communities can use the school facilities.

A TESL teacher was likewise very enthusiastic:

> It would be fantastic if it were the case ... I like to see more heritage language taught in the school system (at this school Mandarin was taught within the school curriculum) — we are just beginning to ... second language in a university does not have to be French, it could be any other community language ... If it is possible, it should be in the school curriculum.

But teachers were also aware of the practical problems of including, say, three to four community languages in the school curriculum. Some of the obvious difficulties were mentioned: recruitment of qualified staff, teaching materials and lack of financial means. Both schools run TESL classes. The newcomers (children joining their families from India, Pakistan, Fiji and Hong Kong), are placed in these classes until they become fluent enough to benefit from the normal class lessons. These students, according to teachers, are seriously handicapped in their academic work. A TESL teacher commented:

> Research has shown that it takes 5–8 years to become proficient in a second language to benefit from academic education ... we don't isolate and teach just English — but other subjects as well. Some students have never been to a school — they have to be taught basic concepts.

Another TESL teacher elaborated:

> To give newcomer immigrants chance to integrate into school routine we have a support service ... after two years they can take 80% of regular classes and 20% support work. Of course a lot depends on what they come in with.

However a TESL teacher was cautious:

> I do approve, but it has to be in the right percentage ... where kids for the 4 or 5 years only learn their own home language, that is detrimental. The major concern with the 'new ones' is English, home language is supplementary to maintain links.

A TESL teacher regretted her decision to use only direct methods of teaching:

> In ESL courses we were not to permit any other language ... all Punjabi children class — I was very firm. We learned in the university that we were not to accept any home language. I have been guilty of that. I now think mother-tongue is very important of one's culture. We have Mandarin taught at school, and I don't know why not Punjabi.

In sum, there was a positive and full support for community language teaching.


## Proficiency of English

### Birmingham

The majority of teachers (18/27) thought that students who were born in Britain and who have attended British schools can manage their secondary school work satisfactorily. But, on further probing, a number admitted (8/27) that their spoken English is of adequate standard, but that their written English is not. A white (male) teacher opined:

> They all communicate very well, but there is a distinct advantage to black and white children. They can use idioms and have richer vocabulary than Muslims kids. Even if they (blacks and whites) are not bright, they can use metaphors, idioms with ease. For instance kids in my class did not know 'thigh' ... they have restricted vocabulary. Even when the kids (Asians) are born here English is still not their first language — of course a lot depends on the home-background. If a family is English-speaking it is alright.

Likewise, doubts were expressed by a white woman primary school teacher:

> Children who were born here ... quite a few are with very little English. It seems to vary ... 5th year girls (primary) were amazingly bad, that they have been through the system and they were born here, I was quite shocked, really. They have not been picked up. They communicate so well

orally, but in their work it was disastrous.

A white teacher in charge of ESL Unit commented: 'I would say up to 80% of children in the mainstream need some sort of language support.'

### Vancouver

All the participants, save three, thought that the students' competence in English is 'normal' as compared with other groups, provided they have had full schooling in Canada. But there was a divergence of viewpoint. A teacher of ESL argued:

> They are a lot in ESL (even if they are born in Canada?). Yes, quite a number ... majority are trapped ... they continue to do so even those who are born here: some excel in maths. It is 5 or 6 years before they pick up English ... but they are still handicapped, I think, when it comes to grasping higher level concepts.

But another ESL teacher had strong reservations:

> They have definitely ... It is a disguised problem — kind of language they have is for inter-personal conversation, and not for academic work. second generation feels no problem — they go to their counsellor, they get by. They are in the mainstream. If they do badly, it is interpreted as a lack of interest in school, low intelligence etc., but generally they don't have language to deal with the complexity of academic subjects.

Schools, in my opinion, should monitor students' standard of English in the main stream and provide support and remedial help where it is needed, otherwise a number of students will definitely under-achieve (see The Way Forward: Schools Council Report, 1981).

## Level of Achievement

### Birmingham

The majority of our sample held the view (16/27) that the performance level of Asian origin students is average to above average. However, some teachers were sceptical. In their view, the performance of Asian children is often compared with that of the white inner-city children (often of lower socio-economic background) and not with that of the middle-class white children. An Asian, male lecturer in education argued:

> It is difficult to say — but their potential is not being realised, this is my

observation. Reasons are: working in English (which is their second language), low expectations of teachers ... white teachers sometimes mock their (students') high expectations and treat them badly.

A white, female head of a multicultural school was very factual in her account:

> We have lifted our tail, but not our head. Only 14% get Grade I or equivalent (CSE). White boys achieve the best and the least, black girls do better than black boys and the Asian sample is too small to generalise.

An Asian, female head was very candid in her observation:

> Achievement levels are mixed. In inner-city areas, teachers appointed are not of good quality — they go in the inner-circle schools when they can't find promotion in the outer-circle schools. Then there are discipline problems ... attitudes are negative. But there are some kids who succeed.

A recent research report (Smith & Tomlinson, 1989) suggests that the performance of Asian students, with the exception of Bangladeshis, is very close to the performance of white students, when social class and other variables are taken into account. But in inner-city schools Asian students, with the exception of Bangladeshis again, have generally performed better than the whites. *The Independent* (8th March, 1990) summarised the Inner London Education Authority (ILEA—now defunct) report with a bold headline 'Indian children best performers in school exams'. The paper goes on to describe the main reason: 'Indian families put pressure on their children to succeed and teachers had high expectations of them'.

## Vancouver

Most of the teachers commented upon the performance level of students; it was described as average to above average. The high achievers were thought to be from the Chinese communities. However, a counsellor commented:

> I don't think you can stereotype a group ... I think 10% have learning disability ... but full range of achievement. I don't think there is any difference compared to other groups.

Another counsellor disagreed:

> Indo-Canadian is like the black Americans; average to below average ... many of the students never work hard to develop their full capacity. It may be that the type of students who attend our school ... the majority come from traditional homes, probably are coloured by their experience (meaning lack of interest in education).

## Racism and Equality of Opportunity

### Birmingham

Most teachers in the sample admitted (24/27) that there is a degree of unintentional racism or ethnocentrism in their schools. A white, female senior teacher elaborated:

> Some teachers should examine their own racist views ... they would be quite horrified to admit that ... some of the games illustrating racism are quite good. Remarks such as... don't behave like a monkey or eat a banana can give offence. Teachers should be careful what they say and never man-handle children; also their expressions and emotional reactions to ethnic food, dress etc. should not offend.

A black, male teacher argued that 'equality of opportunity' is only a slogan as far as the black and Asian students are concerned.

> Yes, they got racism (white teachers). It applies to Asians as well, but they seem to surmount that ... Our kids have to work extra hard. We got to be 100% over the whites. Parents should instil this in their children. No good comparing it with George who is white ... they have to be twice as good.

However, there were a number (3/27) of teachers who dissented from these views. Typical remarks were as follows:

> Teachers are very understanding at our school. They work to the needs of children. We have introduced elements of Islam in our history course. Religious Education is mostly comparative and two ethnic languages are taught. We invite Imam to take prayers in the school. Our parent governors are Muslims and have a real say the way school is run. I am not sure about equality of opportunity in jobs, but here they have it alright.

Some teachers were very positive about their colleagues. An Asian (male) teacher observed:

> I don't think so ... some teachers really love our children. I say to other teachers if we want to educate children, we must win co-operation of parents. A Muslim priest explained to me that he does not want his daughter for mixed swimming, but the headmaster is obstinate and insists that he has the right to force the policy of the school on all children ... then there are problems. I tried to explain to parents we live in England and all children should learn swimming, Why? because we are surrounded by the sea.

All teachers agreed that students are going to face discrimination in jobs. Therefore, they argued that students should be equipped with the necessary academic and social skills to compete in the employment market. However, the means to achieve these ends were somewhat different for individuals.

## Vancouver

Would they enjoy equal opportunity when they leave school? Comments on this question were mixed and varied, but the majority thought that they would face few problems. A teacher commented:

I love to say yes — but I don't think it will happen. (Majority think they will?) ... it is good that they do — but one has to be honest.

A home–school worker:

There won't be any bias, if they got the right qualifications and motivation — they would get fair chance.

Other typical comments of teachers were:

Now there are — but in my generation *no*, the new generation believes in equality.

There is racism against Indian people in Vancouver ... East Indians are doing low grade jobs; Sikh extremists blew up a plane ... this affected the situation. There is prejudice against recently arrived Hong Kong Chinese ... it is acceptable to have immigrants without money, but it is not acceptable that they have more money than we do!!!.

They have to work at it ... more so than the white Canadians, so there is a disparity, but in a lot of areas, if you are qualified, you are an East Indian and female, you are 'in' ... there is positive discrimination. Like 'low' with the native Indians. At gut feeling level you feel 'no', but you won't find enough data to say so.

A counsellor commented:

I would hope — I think so — I won't be sure, I had a student come to me saying he has been rejected from a job because of his racial background.

It seems to me that although most of the teachers and others are optimistic, there is still discrimination in desirable jobs against the visible minorities in Canada. It is interesting to note, however, that the majority of students in our study thought that they would enjoy equal opportunity in the job market. An ethnic minority teacher was very optimistic:

I can say, opportunity is there — it is up to each individual. We have an Indo-Canadian as Vice-Principal, a Japanese-Canadian who is a Principal.

## Social Identity

### Birmingham

Teachers were asked their views on this important matter: Do you think they are Muslims/Sikhs or Asians/Indians or British Muslims? As expected teachers' comments varied a lot: some commented on their religious identities being quite distinctive, others emphasised their 'Britishness', i.e. citizen of the UK, and a few felt that a new term might have to 'be coined' or used: British Asians or British Muslims etc. Here is a selection of the responses:

An Asian woman teacher:

> They are proud of whatever they are ... Muslims, Sikhs. Bengali are concerned with being Bangladeshis ... Yes, I think religion is an important part of their identity.

A white male teacher observed:

> I see them as British — majority were born in this country ... some of them don't appreciate this because their parents (most) hold dual nationalities (Pakistan/British). But they (meaning Muslim boys and girls) emphasise their religion, some may say they are Pakistanis. But they don't realise how British they have become culturally as well: they prefer chips and beans, watch English TV programmes, listen to pop music. Boys are more fashion-conscious ... wear trainers etc.

As an Asian teacher commented:

> They are neither Indians nor British ... I suppose we should call them as they do in Canada, viz: Indo-Canadian. Here I believe equivalent word would be British-Indian/British Sikhs/British-Punjabis etc. They are living in two worlds/cultures ... so it follows they would have bicultural identities.

But British people generally still refer to the second generation as Pakistanis or Indians and some even refer to them as second generation immigrants. Unfortunately these 'labels' can cause a lot of anxiety amongst the young Asians who consider themselves to be bicultural and citizens of this country.

### Vancouver

Teachers' comments were sought on this important point: Are they East Indian? Or are they Indo-Canadian/ Or are they Canadian? Again opinions were mixed as were the labels used to describe the people from the Indian sub-continent. A teacher replied:

> I got my multicultural background, but I shouldn't say I am French/Polish-Canadian, I never use it. East Indians ... in my mind, they are Canadian. I don't think that they are Indo-Canadians, but probably a lot of people do. Chinese in Vancouver are considered immigrants — the pecking order is who is the most recent. It is sad — they (Chinese) built the rail roads. But unfortunately with this onslaught from Hong Kong, they are lumped together. We are certainly not a perfect society.

Another teacher reflected:

> We are all immigrants here, in England white English have been there all the time. So I feel Indo-Canadians have a firmer and securer identity here.

Another teacher commented on the Canadian ''mosaic' type culture:

> But Anglo-Saxon WASPs are still there on the top ... it is not an opinion, it is a fact.

A counsellor commented:

> They are Canadian alright ... Sikh population has achieved power in Alberta. In the Liberal party, they are determining who is going to run as a candidate.

A home–school worker replied:

> They would have Canadian identity, I think it is very hard to call themselves Indian or Canadian. But they accept both cultures. In teen years they are confused — but they work it out. They are more sure.

Another teacher painted a complex picture:

> I have seen and heard both — it is difficult. You are Canadian, yet you bring into the mainstream your home culture. In Vancouver, there is so much diversity. Identity is not an issue — multiple-identity is or I say nested identities.

It seems to me that as the matter stands, the people from the Indian subcontinent are still referred to, both in school and in society at large, as East-Indians. A few thoughtful people in positions of authority are beginning to refer to the community as Indo-Canadian. But Canadian identity itself is such a problematic concept that any further analysis, in the current climate, would not be illuminative. For instance, are the native Indians true Canadians and the rest immigrants? However, the majority of young people consider themselves as Indo-Canadians (see Chapter 2:69).

## Special Problems of Asian Adolescents

### Birmingham

The central purpose of this study was to illuminate those areas of concern which are particularly related to the all-round development of Asian adolescents. Therefore all our interviewees were asked their views on this topic. Many teachers (12/27) commented on the difference of values between home and school. A white, female deputy head crystallised these as follows:

> We teach girls to be independent and critical thinkers, but at home they are taught the virtues of collective responsibility and unquestioning respect to the elders in the family ... naturally this creates tension in the youngsters.

The problem relating to independence versus conformity to family values was mentioned specifically in relation to girls. In early adolescence, for instance, some girls might like to cut their hair and wear make-up against their parents wishes. A woman social worker describes the scene:

> I watch girls at lunch time; they pull up their long skirts, loosen their hair and put lipstick on. They are transformed. Some of them do have boy friends ... others like to look attractive. There are a lot of Asian young men at lunch-time and home-time around school ... they (girls) often pick up the worst aspects of European culture and look cheap.

It was mentioned by some teachers (5/27) that their girl students have been 'pushed' into arranged marriages against their wishes. An Afro-Caribbean male teacher commented:

> This beautiful Asian girl was very unhappy. They won't let her out of her room once in the house after school ... till next morning. They locked her up, she was very upset about this arranged marriage and parents were afraid she might run away.

An Asian woman teacher gave the following insight:

> Parents are very strict ... second-generation have suffered most ... they have double standards — for boys and girls. Some girls when they come home, they have to change into Indian costumes ... shopping they are allowed. But boys can have girl friends ... But I can't generalise, a lot depends on the family.

A social-worker expanded this line of argument:

> Asian parents turn a blind eye to their boys ... (Why?) it is a sexist community. Boys don't often rebel, they have all the traditional advantages. It is

mostly girls who are frustrated ... this runaway Muslim girl said ... I am a Muslim girl born in England, I want to do what my friends do ... (some of whom are Muslims, some whites) go to disco etc. But parents won't agree ... she said: 'this is my life and I want to live it my way'.

However an Afro-Caribbean social-worker was cautious of intervention:

We must be aware of in-built Euro-centric norms and jump in ... we have to be careful of intervention. Girls have to be told of the consequences of their action. They might come to regret it.

A Sikh woman teacher bitterly complained of injustices prevalent in the community:

Women are judged harshly, especially by other women of our community. Gender inequality gets me. It is everywhere. They say she is a lovely girl ... she has united the family. She is a bad girl, because she has split the family ... I don't need a man to look after me, I am sick of hearing this from other women. A lot of educated girls are going away from our culture. They are sick of being treated as second-class citizens.

The social workers recounted a small number of cases of young Asian girls who had run away from home to escape arranged marriages. Here is a typical example:

A Sikh girl ran away at 17. She was in love with an Asian man, but he was a Muslim. He had a job and was very loving. Her parents said No. They ran away and squatted somewhere. Girl's parents wanted me to take care orders ... I understand parents' anxieties as some girls have been exploited by their boyfriends ... pushed into prostitution (how?). Boys had no serious intentions, through blackmail, i.e. they will tell their (girls') families.

However, a number of teachers (14/27) felt that compromise solutions are emerging to this vexed and extremely sensitive problem. A woman Asian teacher argued:

... I am not sure marriages are arranged in the traditional way ... they are getting more and more modified. My parents did not know I would be dating the guy I was going to marry. We had a long engagement. I was committed ... but I could have changed if I didn't like him. A lot of girls (refers to Hindus and Sikhs) do have boyfriends ... parents are beginning to accept the inevitable. Some turn a blind eye.

Some teachers predicted that problems relating to gender equality would hopefully be resolved by the third-generation young people.

**Vancouver**

Again matters raised by our respondents mainly relate to girls' behaviour and adjustment at school. It is quite well known now both through empirical researches (Ghuman, 1975) and cumulative professional experience that people from the Indian sub-continent, generally, prefer boys to girls, give more freedom and opportunities to boys than girls and are more protective towards their girls. It should, however, be noted that there are considerable variations: religion, caste-class, region, educational background, kinship groupings and rural/urban background all have significant influence on whether parents hold a traditional or modern outlook on gender equality. A teacher reinforced and expanded:

> It all depends from the home they come from, if they come from a tradi-tional home, they are really torn between two cultures. They can become very depressed — they can't do things which other kids can do. Rather than participating in school activities, they berry pick or do newspaper rounds — help cooking at home ... though some girls do stay (now) in school to do vocational courses.

Another teacher contradicted this observation:

> No, I don't think so — very similar — sometimes I think they are more protective of their daughters than sons — I sense that some other groups do the same.

A counsellor agreed with this view:

> Their concerns are very similar to other parents I have not experienced any-thing special ... but there is a degree of stereotyping ... there are other communities who have this protective outlook especially towards girls.

An ESL teacher had a different perspective on the issue:

> This is a difficult one — who is to say ... East Indian should be more Western? They are caught between two cultures ... if I were to move to England, I won't fit in. Parents are trying ... Kaur and Singh have been dropped ... they have cut their hair. (Kaur and Singh are middle names of Sikh girls and boys respectively).

A counsellor further elaborated:

> Most of the problems I have dealt with are the girls' — some girls tend to skip school, they are expected to be home after school — girls get very dis-enchanted that they are not allowed to date — whereas Canadian students can, in some cases, they sneak off and have boyfriends. Some of them are very afraid of their families, especially fathers ... boys have privileges; there doesn't seem to be any problem with them dating white girls — they are certainly allowed.

A home–school worker provided another perspective:

> It is a problem — the moment they come to school, they go to the washrooms. Put make-up on, untie their hair. When they go home — they braid it back ... I have experienced this many times. I don't blame them — they like to be like everybody else. At home parents are too strict — there should be a medium way — teachers encourage them to be independent.

Here we have a crystallisation of the problem: individual orientation of the Canadian society as represented by the teachers versus the collective orientation of the Punjabi way of life; only compromises can work in this difficult situation. For instance, in Britain, Asian youngsters organise discos and 'Bhangrapop' on Saturdays in the afternoon rather than in the evening with the approval of their parents.

Another type of problem is related to the wearing of appropriate clothes for lessons in PE and swimming, but according to home–school workers these have been resolved. Likewise some parents are now willing for their daughters to stay after school to participate in games. Another concern of parents according to a home–school worker is:

> System is too liberal — there is not enough discipline. This is the main reason why a lot of parents don't allow their girls to go on school trips.

## Perceived Concerns of Parents

### Birmingham

It is generally believed that Asian parents have a very high regard for education. Partly it springs from the legacy of the British Raj in India. Indians could aspire to get into civil, military and other government jobs provided they had gone through the English-styled schools and obtained certificates and diplomas from the British set-up colleges and universities. Education was considered to be a means of social mobility. One of the principal reasons behind the immigration of Asians was to achieve a higher standard and status in life by sending their children to English schools. The teachers, on the whole, agreed with the above observations. We can illustrate it through suitable extracts. An Asian male deputy head teacher of a multicultural school:

> I get good co-operation from parents ... attendance at parents' evening is over 80%. They cook ethnic food, decorate the school hall, sew costume. They are marvellous. I have a home–school liaison teacher. He can speak

three Asian languages and has built up very good links with parents.

A male community language teacher had a slightly different perspective:

> Asian parents give good support. But they have Indian mentality — leave education to the teachers and schools ... better not interfere or annoy teachers. But they would like more home-work and strict discipline and compulsory uniform.

A male Afro-Caribbean teacher gave this very interesting account:

> I say I will give an hour during lunch ... West Indian children won't come, Asians would. I do private tuition with them ... they are 10 minutes earlier and leave 10 minutes late. But West Indians would come 10–20 minutes late and want to leave early to watch a football match on the TV. I am talking from my practical experience ... Asian parents are more tuned to the system. On parents' day you will meet white and Asian parents, few blacks.

However, a number of teachers mentioned the difficulties which Asian parents face in developing closer links with schools. A female headteacher of a multicultural secondary special school:

> ... difficult to develop partnership with my parents and that has been one of the problems: parental involvement. For them language and concepts used are different and difficult. I have to educate the parents. My school is welcoming, but parents want an open house ... immediate attention. The English head may not do it, meet them at the same platform, give equal respect. I invite parents, cook food on premises, sit side by side with them.

Previous researchers have commented upon the problems which the Asian parents face in forming closer links with schools (Tomlinson, 1984; Ghuman, 1980). Poor spoken English is the chief reason, shift work is another problem and lack of confidence to approach teachers and others in authority is also a salient factor.

## Vancouver

Two teachers mentioned parents' anxiety over their children's continued placement in the ESL stream. One teacher was concerned that parents think their children are not getting enough regular homework and that too much time is spent on art, music, drama and the like. A counsellor commented:

> ... Parents' concerns are very much with their education courses, ESL programme, and being integrated into the main stream.

An ESL teacher observed:

> Parents from traditional societies think that the North American system is too lax — less discipline etc. ... this is quite common in America where Korean and Vietnamese complain about the homework and lack of rote learning.

Most parents in the catchment area are from the traditional farming background and do not really appreciate the importance of active participation in students' school life. This problem was highlighted by the home–school workers: 'Very few parents take part (school sponsored activities) — they say we have no contribution to make'. Another important factor is the lack of knowledge of spoken English; a lot feel embarrassed that their accents would not be understood by the teacher (see next chapter for details).

A 'complaint' made by a home–school worker was that nearly all Punjabi families are caught up in the material well-being at the expense of the education of their children:

> Wives and husbands are busy around the clock — women get jobs as dishwashers and in laundries and men work in saw mills — this way children get neglected. Some start going out to the McDonalds or meet friends on the road. Parents work very hard to pay off mortgages. They say work for seven or eight years — then they would enjoy the children and TV — but it is too late. Children have grown up and become independent. Parents not getting involved with their schooling is the biggest drawback — they get involved when it is too late.

Another reason for not getting actively involved is that on the Indian subcontinent it is considered rude and interfering ('busybodies') if parents go to school often to enquire about their youngsters' progress.

As the parents attended school in India, they have this 'mental set' that education is in the province of teachers and schools, and it is not their business to interfere. A report evaluating the multicultural policies of the Vancouver School Board found this to be the case with the Indo-Canadian parents (Fisher & Echols, 1989: 61-3).

## Separate Schools

### Birmingham

Some sections of the ethnic communities, particularly the Muslims, believe that the needs of their children would be best served in separate religious schools. Teachers' opinions were divided on this issue. Most Asian (10/15) teachers felt that ethnic minorities should enjoy the same rights and privileges as the established religious minorities do, for example the Jews and Roman Catholics. But others felt that the setting up of separate schools would probably encourage segregation and educationally disadvantage children. Comments like 'I don't support it, they have to learn to live together', were typical of the responses. But a detailed comment of an Asian male lecturer is illuminating:

> My own view is they will become ghetto schools and this would have a negative effect, and we haven't got a Black University ... and it is against integration. We should stay within the mainstream and demand our just rights, like single sex schools. Adolescence is a vulnerable period and needs special care ... but it doesn't mean we need separate schools.

### Vancouver

All the teachers in the study were in favour of separate schools for religious purposes, if the communities so wished. A woman teacher commented:

> It is a free country ... they have the same rights as the Roman Catholics. The Sikhs have started a Khalsa high school in Vancouver ... there is no restriction.

# Multicultural Education

### Birmingham

The Swann Committee's report (Swann, 1985) on multicultural education made wide-ranging recommendations. The important new perspective put forward by the committee was that schools, irrespective of their ethnic intake, should include basic principles of multiculturalism in their formal and informal curriculum. The reason given to support this stance was that all students need to be aware of the cultural diversity of British society and should learn tolerance and respect for cultures for other than their own.

The majority of teachers (20/27) in our sample believed that there has not been a concerted attempt to implement the recommendations of the Swann Report on multi-cultural education. An Asian (male) teacher commented:

> We have a multicultural society, but monocultural curriculum. There is little in RE and History ... it is tokenism. Things haven't changed that much.

All teachers felt that it was equally important for all white schools to have multicultural curicula. A (male) teacher of Punjabi observed:

> White children should know about our culture ... enjoy our food and dress, know our religion and history. It is only happening in some black schools ... it should be in all schools.

The comments of white teachers were also in favour of curriculum change. A white (female) ESL teacher:

> I am not an idealist as I used to be ... it is not widespread, it should be. Reality is different. You would have thought it would be the norm ... it all depends on particular schools. Changes are not even tokenistic in some places. I find it quite depressing.

Most teachers (20/27) took the line that multicultural education means a good education and that it is not a separate subject or issue. A white woman teacher observed:

> We should use the experience which children bring into the school. This is supposed to be an important psychological principle which is the basis of sound classroom practice.

The introduction of the National Curriculum in British schools, according to our respondents, has further marginalised multicultural education. Such a view is also expressed by academics in the field of multicultural education (Tomlinson, 1991; Troyna, 1990).


**Vancouver**

The Vancouver schools board has a clear policy on multicultural education, therefore it was thought interesting to explore the views and feelings of the participants. We can let the respondents speak for themselves. A committed teacher reasoned:

> Our policy aim is to involve all students, as far as possible, and accommodate new ideas if we can't change the curriculum. We do have celebrations, feast days are broadcast over the speakers — offer congratulations, we have a multi-cultural week in Canada and in schools. We would have an open house — encourage all the departments to take part. Our demonstration tend to be one night or one week. We would like to be consistent — we have speakers come. Sari demonstration for the sewing class etc. Parents are very supportive.

An ethnic home–school worker:

> Most teachers are sympathetic to multicultural education — there are a few

who don't support ... they (teachers) are becoming more optimistic. Mandarin is taught in school, for example, Sikh kids don't have long hair (apart from few) or turbans, they feel ostracised. But we have a video Gurdip Singh his life etc., there are multicultural books by Kehoe ...

Sikh students do not feel easy wearing turbans is a theme of another teacher, who comments:

Kids tend to be curious of this student's turban — does he wash his hair etc. So one day when this Sikh boy was absent from my class, I discussed with them the basic points of Sikh religion and explained the importance of turban ... students have been better since then.

Another teacher gave a cautious welcome:

What does it mean exactly? I think it is a wonderful idea, but here in Canada we are having a difficult time even French and English are not getting along. We can't do anything more complex ... we are not good at it, but impetus behind is good ... Schools are in danger of doing too many things ... then be in danger of not doing them very well.

But some teachers were enthusiastic:

I believe, here multicultural education is an issue ... validates the fact we come from different backgrounds and that should be appreciated; the majority of staff are for ME, my biggest disagreement is what form ME should take? I see it as a museum piece type ... food, dress. We have to get behind and do art, history and symbols of other cultures ... it should be a part of the whole school curriculum.

A woman teacher had an interesting experience on multicultural education:

I was involved in multicultural camp week. This Indian girl's parents won't let her go. I have to give my word that I would be responsible, so he let her attend the camp. I learnt a lot through practical activities and so did the students ... Who is to say: East Indians should become more Western? Kids are caught between two cultures; if I were to move to England, I won't fit in. But parents are trying — they have dropped 'Kaur' and 'Singh' from names, cut hair etc. Schools should meet half way.

Here is an example of a teacher who doesn't really believe in multicultural education, but believes in meeting special needs of ethnic minorities:

We have a multicultural day every year, school and staff participate. They (teachers) don't feel it is an issue. It divides them (kids). But we can't work without the home–school worker ... a great help.

A view of another committed counsellor is worth quoting:

> It is an exciting idea — it is wonderful. I like mixing with different people. Wonderful for kids. Enjoy ethnic food — like sharing religious ideas and exchanging views with others.

Thus we have a full range of opinions, from tokenism to 'special needs' notion, through to permeation of multicultural education in the school curriculum. From my own subjective experience of the schools in Vancouver, I feel the schools are in the very early stage of introducing multicultural education. There are staff committees to co-ordinate multicultural education activities, but I think they have a lot of work to do if they want to carry the majority of staff with them. Likewise, there is a need to have materials on the Indo-Canadian in the library and resources centre: books on ethnic religion, history, literature, arts, music and the like should be on the shelves of all school libraries. Then there is the uphill task of persuading subject teachers to include intercultural themes in their syllabuses.

## Conclusions

All the teachers and other respondents in Birmingham and Vancouver supported the students' desire to learn their community's language. As regards the provisions for the teaching of 'ethnic' languages, there were differences of opinion. On the whole, the Asian teachers tended to support the policy of teaching these languages within the curriculum, whereas the white teachers were either lukewarm or against this practice. The chief reason given was that it would take valuable time which could otherwise be spent on the teaching of English, which most students need to realise their full academic potential. Also some teachers thought it should be the responsibility of the ethnic communities — as is the case with the more established communities of Poles and Jews.

In Vancouver, teachers thought it would pose too many practical problems, namely recruitment of suitably qualified teachers, material resources, and unrealistic demands on the already overloaded school curriculum. The following comment from the evaluation report of the Vancouver School Board's race relations policy (Fisher & Echols, 1989: 110) is also relevant:

> The major problem of the HLP (Heritage Language Programme) from the schools' point of view has been the space — sharing in classrooms. ... The major complaint of HLP teachers and co-ordinators is the lack of classroom space which leads to larger classes and makeshift teaching areas.

All the respondents also agreed that Asian students should be made to feel proud of their home cultures. But grave doubts were expressed, mainly by the white teachers, regarding the predicament of girls who have severe restrictions placed on their 'freedoms' and are often denied opportunities for further education. Also some disquiet was expressed over arranged marriages, particularly the ones organised by parents in India/Pakistan without the consent of girls.

The perceived concerns of parents relate to excessive freedom in schools, lack of homework and the spending of too much time on non-essential subjects. Some teachers, both in Birmingham and Vancouver, expressed their worries that parents tend to have unrealistic aspirations for their youngsters:

> ...They all want them to be doctors and engineers, even when the ability and potential is not there.

As regards students' bicultural outlooks, the Canadian sample was wholeheartedly committed and wished to promote bicultural identities actively. However, the British sample was not clear; Asian teachers felt that young people would be obliged to accept their home-identities e.g. Indian or Pakistani or a religious identity e.g. Muslim/Sikh.

The white teachers argued that perhaps their core identities would be based on their religion, but that their social identities would be mixture of the two i.e. bicultural. It may be interesting to note that in Canada 'hyphenated' description of ethnics is quite common, e.g. Indo-Canadian etc., whereas in Britain it is rare ... the common terms used are Asians or Afro-Caribbeans or Chinese.

Teachers in both cities supported the multicultural initiatives, but were less sure how the principles of multiculturalism can be incorporated into their subjects at secondary level. This is confirmed by the Vancouver School Board evaluation report (Fisher & Echols, 1989: 95).

> Some teachers in our field-work schools stated what appears to be a widely held view that multicultural material simply does not fit under the rubric of most high school subjects. Teachers talked about the lack of any 'particular application' or of 'specific utility' of these materials for what they perceived to be their primary task as subject specialist.

It became quite clear during the course of this research that the schools, in both cities, have come a long way in meeting the needs of students in various ways. But as regards the change in content of various subject areas to reflect the diversity of cultures, there has been a little progress. A comment of an Asian male teacher is revealing and sums up the situation:

> Curriculum is still based on the Euro-centric view of the world; other cultures are brought in, but only as an afterthought. You have to recruit more ethnic teachers with high qualifications and the right attitudes to bring about a change.

# 4 Parents' Dilemma

Some teachers (not all) could be more sensitive. They say to our daughters your parents are your jailors! This they justify on human rights. But we can't give up all our customs. I say keep the right balance (between the home and the school values). We think the best for our children — not for our own ego (A Sikh parent in Vancouver).

In the Chapter 1, a brief description of Asian immigrants to Britain and Canada was given so that the concerns and anxieties of young people of Asian origins could be fully understood in a proper context. In the concluding discussion on background information and the settlement patterns, it was stated that their aspirations were modest, and that they had realised most of their pressing needs namely finding a job, owning a house and uniting their families in their country of domicile (Chapter 1: 20). Furthermore it was argued that their identities were, and are, firmly rooted in their religion and culture. They felt secure and at ease with their achievements.

However, their aspirations for their children were and are high. They had great regard for the English system of education and believed that it would provide their young people with sound academic qualifications and language skills to secure jobs with better prospects. Their perceptions were based on their experiences of the British Raj, when an English-educated elite (Ghandi, Nehru, Jinnah) not only led the freedom movement but also got plum jobs in the Indian Civil Service, medicine, law and education. English qualifications were a passport to a good job, fame, respect and a bright future. It is within this context that we have to examine their attitudes on educational and social matters relating to young people's bicultural identities and educational progress.

## Samples

### Birmingham

Some 30 parents living in the catchment area of three schools, where research on young people was carried out, were contacted through teachers and personal contacts. In the event only 14 parents agreed to take part due to a variety of reasons, the chief one being that they were too busy and they had not much to say.

Another 10 parents, known through personal and professional contacts, were included for interview to make our sample viable for analysis and discussion. The details of the sample are given in Table 4.1.

**Table 4.1** Details of parents' sample from Birmingham

| Interviews | Men = 16 | Women = 4 | Families = 4 | Total 24 |
|---|---|---|---|---|
| Age in Years | 35–40 | 41–45 | 46–55 | |
| | 5 | 16 | 3 | |
| Education | Primary | Secondary | Higher | |
| | 4 | 11 | 9 | |
| Years of stay | 10–15 | 16–20 | 21+ | |
| | 5 | 16 | 3 | |
| Occupation | Manual | Non-manual | | |
| | 12 | 12 | | |
| Family | Nuclear | Extended | Nuclear + Grandparents | |
| | 7 | 1 | 16 | |
| Children at school | Primary | Secondary | | |
| | 8 | 24 | | |
| Religion | Sikhs | Hindus | Muslims | |
| | 10 | 8 | 6 | |
| Home language | Punjabi/Urdu/ | English | Mixture of English/Hindi Punjabi etc | |
| | 8 | 6 | 10 | |
| Children born in England | Yes | No | | |
| | 24 | 0 | | |

**Vancouver**

I did not use schools to make contact with parents as the principals and the teaching staff had already given a lot of their time and energy. Parents were approached through kinship networks, Gurudawaras and temples. In all, 26 parents living in Vancouver, Surrey and Abbotsford were interviewed. However, only four parents were from the schools where I interviewed the young people and used the bicultural scale. Details of the sample are given in Table 4.2.

**Table 4.2** Details of parents' sample from Vancouver

| Interviews | Men | Women | Families | Total |
|---|---|---|---|---|
| | 14 | 2 | 10 | 26 |
| Age in Years | 30–35 | 36-40 | 41–45 | |
| | 4 | 16 | 6 | |
| Education | Primary | Secondary | Further & Higher | |
| | 6 | 12 | 8 | |
| Years of stay | 10–15 | 16–20 | 21+ | |
| in Canada | 5 | 16 | 5 | |
| Occupation | Manual | Non-Manual | | |
| | 20 | 6 | | |
| Family | Extended | Nuclear | Nuclear+Grandparents | |
| | 0 | 6 | 20 | |
| Children at | Elementary | Secondary | | |
| School | 8 | 18 | | |
| Religion | Sikhs | Hindus | No practising religion | |
| | 14 | 8 | 4 | |
| Home language | Punjabis/Hindi | English | English/Punjabi–Hindi mixed | |
| | 12 | 8 | 4 | |
| Children born | | | | |
| in Canada | Yes | No | | |
| | 26 | 0 | | |

A number of points emerge from the data which are significant: most families are nuclear, the majority of fathers are manual workers — nearly all in sawmills, and a number had higher education from the country of origin (but these were not recognised as equivalent to the British Columbian Standards). For instance, a mother held an MA degree in Politics and a father was a Bachelor of Science — yet both of them were working in factories doing manual jobs.

## Methodology

Parents' views were gained through semi-structured interviews, which were conducted in their homes. The details of this method are given in Chapter 1, but two points need emphasising. Asian parents tend to be guarded and even suspicious of people in authority. This is based on their experiences of Indo-Pakistani bureaucrats who are often wasteful and interfering. Secondly, Asian parents are more likely to give those responses which, in their opinion, would please the interviewer and, thereby, minimise a possible conflict (see Ghuman, 1980; Ghuman & Gallop, 1981).

To minimise the effect of these factors, it was considered very important to win the full confidence of parents by explaining to them the objectives of the enquiry. A preliminary social visit, prior to the full interview, was deemed necessary to gain their co-operation and increase the reliability of our interview. The majority of parents (35/50) chose to talk in their mother-tongue, i.e. Punjabi/Urdu/Hindi — which I can speak and write very well. A small number of parents (5/50) did not want me to audio-record their conversation; in such cases detailed notes were taken and impressions added after the interviews. Summaries of parents' responses are presented in Tables 4.3 and 4.4.

**Table 4.3** Summary of parents' responses (Birmingham)

|  | Approve | Don't approve | No opinion |
|---|---|---|---|
| Co-education | 16 | 8 | — |
| School discipline | 12 | 12 | — |
| School curriculum | 4 | 4 | 16 |
|  | *Satisfied* | *Not satisfied* | *No opinion* |
| Home work | 12 | 12 | — |
|  | *Yes* | *No* | *Don't know/No opinion* |
| Home language should be taught at school | 22 | — | 2 |
| Prejudice at school | 2 | 22 | — |
| Equality with whites in jobs | — | 24 | — |
| Equality of treatment of boys and girls | 16 | 8 | — |
| Help with homework | 4 | 20 | — |
| Visit school on parents' day | 22 | 2 | — |
| Satisfied with education and schooling | 20 | 4 | — |
|  | *Whites/Black/Others* | | *Asians only* |
| Choice of friends | 24 | | — |
|  | *Mixed* | *British* | *Indian/Pakistani* |
| Identity | 12 | 6 | 6 |

**Table 4.4** Summary of parents' responses (Vancouver)

| | Approve | Don't approve | No opinion |
|---|---|---|---|
| Co-education | 26 | — | — |
| School discipline | 20 | 6 | — |
| School curriculum | 4 | — | 22 |
| | Satisfied | Not satisfied | No opinion |
| Homework | 24 | 2 | — |
| | Yes | No | No opinion |
| Home language should be taught at school | 20 | 6 | — |
| Home language should be taught by community arrangements | 26 | — | — |
| Prejudice at school | — | 26 | — |
| Equality with whites in Jobs | 12 | 14 | — |
| Equality of treatment of boys and girls | 22 | 4 | — |
| Help with homework | 6 | 20 | — |
| Visit school on parents' day | 20 | 6 | — |
| Satisfied with education and schooling | 24 | 2 | — |
| | Indo-Canadian | | Whites/Others |
| Choice of friends | 2 | | 24 |
| | Canadian | Indo-Canadian | Others |
| Identity | 6 | 20 | — |

## Overall Pattern

The discussion on the opinions of the two samples on various aspects of educational and social issues is integrated to save repetition and enhance readability of the text. It is instructive, firstly, to compare the two samples. The Vancouver sample does not include any Muslim parents as there were no young people of Muslim families in the schools where I conducted the research. The other important difference relates to the occupational status; the Birmingham sample has 50% parents in manual jobs whereas the Vancouver sample has 77.1%.

The comparison between the two samples on their responses to various aspects of social and educational matters is illuminating. The Canadian sample, as compared to the Birmingham, is supportive of co-education and school discipline and is satisfied with the homework situation and schooling of its sons and daughters in general. Also the Canadian parents feel their young people to have a distinct Indo-Canadian identity and a significant proportion (46%) believe that their youngsters would be treated as well as the whites when they seek employment. But all the parents feel that community languages should be taught by the schools and that the schools which their children attend are free of racial prejudice. The latter finding is a very encouraging sign of parents' trust in teachers and schools.

## Educational Background of Parents

All the parents had their schooling/education in the country of origin, e.g. Pakistan and India. Therefore it was considered important to know their personal experiences on the matter as these are likely to colour their perceptions and evaluation of educational issues in their country of domicile.

Most parents (45/50) thought that the education which they received was based on rather hard regimes, consisted of rote learning and general fear of their teachers. The following two responses are typical. A Sikh trade union official (Vancouver) graphically narrated:

> Teachers in India are viewed as scary things; even our parents used to say if you don't listen to us, I am going to talk to your teacher and that used to scare the pants off us. They beat us up; we were demoralised. Teacher sitting as a dictator on a chair and we on the ground.

A Muslim white-collar worker (Birmingham) had a similar experience:

> I have to grow out of the hard discipline; it didn't teach us anything. I came from Gujrat (Pakistan). I don't like that discipline. Teacher would say: bring your homework; if not you were caned regularly. We were caned a lot. A lot of kids actually dropped out because of this.

However, some parents (5/50) thought there were some good points in the system. A Sikh car mechanic and his social worker wife (Vancouver) commented:

> In India they are strict ... otherwise it is good. Most children learn to read and write quickly. They emphasise the 3R's, which is very good.

A Hindu primary school teacher (Birmingham) had a different angle:

In Punjab children respect their teachers, but this is not the case here. There is more discipline and children are pushed — sometimes through fear. Arithmetic is taught as a bitter pill. Standards are higher in mental arithmetic.

Besides discipline, respect for teachers and higher standards in arithmetic, parents also mentioned the high value placed on education by the community. Education was mentioned by the famous writer Naipaul (1991) as the key to social mobility, knowledge (Ghián) and enlightenment.

It is interesting to note that in England and Wales, there is a major shift of policy on the teaching of the 3Rs in primary schools. Spelling and tables are now considered to be very important in the National Curriculum. The Secretary of State for Education has asked the examining boards, and they have complied, to award 5% of the total marks for good spelling.

## Discipline

Opinions on this topic ranged from strong approval through mild support to the rejection of a 'laissez faire' approach to teaching. A Hindu shopkeeper (Birmingham) approves of discipline:

Discipline is quite good in my children's school ... they enjoy their freedom in a good framework. But on the whole teachers should be more strict.

The point about strictness is also echoed by a parent (a Sikh technician) in Vancouver:

According to us it is lax; students don't respect their teachers. I saw a class room like a circus — kids shouting abuses etc. For children it can become normal, but not for me. I don't like it.

Further analysis of responses showed that parents were careful not to make wild generalisations, but based their comments on actual experiences of schools which their children attended. Parental attitudes on discipline emerging from the present research are supportive of the findings of my previous studies with Asian parents (Ghuman, 1980; Ghuman & Gallop, 1981). It was not thought feasible to make comparisons between the Hindu and Muslim parents as the numbers are small. But in our research (Ghuman & Gallop, 1981), we found Muslim parents to prefer stricter disciplining of their youngsters as compared to the Hindus.

Discipline is a very topical issue in Britain. The newly appointed Secretary of State for Education has shown his concern over poor discipline in schools and has advocated the importance of the religious/moral values of the home in halting the deteriorating trend.

## School Curriculum

The majority of parents (38/50) in both cities are not knowledgeable about the schools' activities in this area. In England and Wales, a new national curriculum has been introduced in 1988 which, at least notionally, requires parents' active involvement. But even well-educated parents in our sample admitted ignorance on the nature of the school curriculum. A Muslim office worker (Birmingham) expressed his opinion:

> My daughter was going to have exams at the age of 7. I don't know exact details — teachers are to work to that. Teachers are not to construct their own syllabuses. I think teachers should have flexibility, but I am not an expert.

A trade union official (Vancouver) had similar comments:

> I am not in a good position to answer this question. I am not involved in the school that much. Curriculum is affected by the government policies … when school system is run as a business, then it is distorted.

A community leader from Vancouver had a different stance on the matter:

> Over 90% of parents are of a village background — they have problems with spoken English. You can't expect them to know about curriculum.

In our previous research (Ghuman & Gallop, 1981), we found Muslim parents objecting to the teaching of non-academic subjects. Similar views were expressed by three Muslim parents. A shopkeeper argued:

> In our Islamic religion, music, dancing are prohibited. In schools here there are music, dancing, movement, drama, sports — I don't mind sports so much, but I feel it would have been better if schools had religious instruction instead of music, singing and dancing.

Such attitudes probably explain some of the Muslim parents' clamour, in the UK, to establish separate schools, especially for girls.

## Co-education

All the parents in the Vancouver sample supported the mixed schooling of boys and girls. A Sikh journalist (Vancouver) summarised the benefits as follows:

> Co-education is a good thing … boys and girls learn to work together; and this they must do to live in a Canadian society.

Likewise the majority of parents (16/24) in the Birmingham group approved of co-education. A muslim clerical worker (Birmingham) argued:

> No, I don't mind. No problem. But I know a lot of parents who do. The argument is that girls do better in all-girls school. Also it may be they like to protect their daughters. Pakistani community particularly would like to see girls-only schools.'

Our sample is too small to draw any firm conclusion regarding the difference of opinion between the Muslims and other communities, but in our previous research (Ghuman & Gallop, 1981) we found the Muslim parents to be in favour of single-sex schools. The reasons given are the same as articulated by a Muslim non-manual worker (Birmingham):

> My own view is they should not be mixed schools. I am in favour of separate schools. Kids begin to go wrong in their adolescent years. But people are compelled to send them to mixed schools; there should be a choice. I know a lot of Muslim parents who feel this way.

A Muslim research worker, Mrs Shaik, in Manchester (Shaikh & Kelly, 1989) found that nearly half the parents studied were in favour of separate schools, but only a quarter of the girls in the sample supported such a move. There appears to be an increasing demand for voluntary-aided separate schools for boys and girls by the Muslim communities in the UK. Whether the government approves of these new single-sex Islamic schools is a matter of great importance to the Muslims (Times Education Supplement, 8th May, 1992: 2).

## Community Languages (Heritage Languages)

Asian parents view this area with the utmost concern (Bhachu, 1985c). Asian languages are very much tied to the religious consciousness and are also an important tool for social intercourse and solidarity. For instance, Punjabi, written in Gurmukhi script, is the language of 'Granth Sahib' — the religious text of the Sikhs. Without the written knowledge of Punjabi, children would be unable to read the original text. All the parents strongly argued for the retention of community languages. A Hindu supermarket owner explained (Birmingham):

> We speak both Punjabi and Hindi at home. I am a staunch believer that my kids must understand these languages. But they can't read or write, which is a pity.

On the question of where the languages should be taught, there was divergence of opinion. The majority (42/50) thought it should be part of the school curriculum. A Sikh writer (Vancouver) argued:

> I sent my children to the Punjabi school. They did not like the atmosphere and gave up. I think where possible, Punjabi should be included in the school syllabus, otherwise it will die. Certainly in the written form, anyway.

The most repeated argument was that the languages should be taught as other modern languages are within the school curriculum and all children should be encouraged to learn Asian languages. A Muslim skilled worker (Birmingham) explained:

> I teach Urdu part-time at school. But it is after school. I say: why it can't be during the school day? Children will respect it and be motivated.

A Sikh couple (Vancouver) expressed a similar view:

> Like French, it should be introduced as a second language. My daughter has done French. We say it could be any other community language.

However, there were some parents (8/50) who thought the teaching of community languages (heritage languages) should be the responsibility of the concerned community and not that of the schools. A Sikh housewife (Birmingham) was very convinced:

> No, why should schools do that? Other ethnic minorities have been able to preserve their languages. Why shouldn't we be able to do it? It is up to us — the home and community. Definitely.

A Sikh accountant (Birmingham) went even further in denouncing moves by schools to undertake such a role:

> What is the use anyway? Good education is about jobs. Learning Hindi/Urdu is not relevant. I would say concentrate on world knowledge. Learning of a mother-tongue can be a hobby. My son doesn't speak Punjabi, it is our fault, not schools. First onus is on parents.

From the interview data, it emerged that, on the whole, Muslim parents are more strict and concerned about the learning of Urdu (which is often not their spoken home language — this tends to be Punjabi) and even Arabic. A Sikh part-time teacher of Punjabi explained:

> There is a sort of imperialism about Asian languages. Most Muslim parents think that Urdu is the best language to learn — it came from the Moghuls who were rulers of India for two centuries — though they speak Punjabi at home. From my own experience, I can say Muslim parents are keener than the Hindus and Sikhs. They are very determined that their youngsters should learn Urdu and also Arabic. Their weekend schools are very well attended.

Other researchers (Bhachu, 1985c; Smith & Tomlinson, 1989) have noted that a large majority of Asian parents would like the teaching of the mother-tongue, where possible to be within the school curriculum. Smith & Tomlinson (1989: 107) conclude their discussion on community language with the recommendation:

> From the extensive provision of minority languages outside schools, it is clear that there would be a substantial demand for these subjects if schools could offer them. One of the most important steps that schools can take towards a multicultural education policy is to develop the teaching of Asian languages and literature within the framework of the National Curriculum.

From my observations both in Canada and the UK, it seems that the week-end community schools are not very popular with the youngsters and are poorly attended. There are many reasons for this; the main one being the lack of proper facilities and resources. Schools are often held in rundown, noisy, make-shift buildings and books and other illustrative materials are imported from India/China and these do not capture the hearts and minds of children. The related problem is that the youngsters do not perceive their community's language as of a high status that deserves their attention. It is not included in the school programmes and its use is limited. Therefore, the schools should consider very seriously including the teaching of community languages in their curricula. Such language programmes should be open to all students and 'language' qualifications thereby gained in secondary/high schools should be recognised by the universities and other professional bodies. Otherwise there is a dark future in store for ethnic languages.

# Religious Education

The problems relating to the teaching of religions do not arise in Canada as the schools are run on a secular basis. Therefore, the discussion on this topic is under two separate headings: Vancouver and Birmingham.

## Vancouver

Most parents felt that it is up to them and their community to provide instruction in religion. A Sikh woman home-school worker explained:

> Schools don't teach RE. I do it at home. I have books and I teach them. We go to Gurudwara. My son goes and pays respect to the holy book and then goes in the yard and plays with his friends. He likes langar (meal from a free kitchen) and 'parsad' from the priest.

A response from an Hindu clerical worker is along similar lines:

> Schools in Canada don't teach religion. It can become so controversial. I
> think it is right. We try to teach our kids the basis of our religion. We have
> a shrine at home. We read Gita and sometimes have 'Katha' (sermons) at
> home.

## Birmingham

In Britain, the 'religious question' has posed many problems. According to
the 1944 and 1988 Acts of Education, all maintained schools should have a
morning assembly in the mainstream religion Christianity; though parents have
the right to withdraw their children from assembly. In addition, schools are also
obliged to teach Religious Education (RE) as a compulsory subject.

Stuart Maclure (1988: 19) makes a poignant commentary on the 1988
Education Act:

> For many it seemed paradoxical that the 'Christian' character of religious
> education and religious worship in schools was being restated and
> enshrined in law at a time when the school population was more multi-faith
> than ever before. But it was seen as a paradox which the schools could live
> with. It seemed unlikely that the enforcement of the new law would be any
> more effective than had been the enforcement of compulsory religious
> instruction and worship in the 1944 Act.

The schools which we have studied have adopted a 'comparative
approach': the basic tenets of the major world religions are taught with the aim
of promoting mutual tolerance and respect. Morning assemblies are also multi-
faith and priests of different faiths are invited to talk to students on some aspects
of their religion.

All the parents in our research affirmed the value of their religion in main-
taining their cultural identity; it was referred to as the core factor. A Sikh
chemist (Birmingham) explained:

> Religion binds us together, especially when we are away from our home
> land. My children can read the holy texts; we have them at home. Through
> these they have learnt our history, achievements and the sacrifices which
> the gurus made for the Sikh panth.

Likewise a Muslim factory worker (Birmingham) affirmed:

> For us the Koran is the foundation of all knowledge... it guides us in all
> walks of life: birth, onset of puberty, marriages, divorce, property rights,

criminal and everything else. We have 500 mosques in Birmingham. There is so much need. Now during Ramadan we are supposed to pray five times a day; still there are not enough mosques.

On the question of youngsters' religious education, most parents (19/24) thought that as long as schools do not undermine their religion and 'brainwash' their children with Christianity, they (parents) along with the community would be responsible for the religious growth of their children. A Hindu clerical worker (Birmingham) expressed it like this:

Schools can't have resources to teach religions. I am quite happy that my son goes to Gita Mandir to learn Hindi and religious teachings of the Gita. Let schools get on with the academic side, I can take care of my religion and language.

Muslim parents, generally, feel strongly for the teaching of Islam (Anwar, 1988); this was confirmed by the Muslim, Hindu and Sikh parents alike. A Muslim restaurant owner (Birmingham) elaborated:

We really need separate schools to bring up our children the Islamic way. But failing that, we have to make arrangements for our children to attend Madrassas at Mosques to learn Arabic and the Koran. My son and daughter go on Fridays and Sundays. I read to them the Koran. My son fasts during the Ramadan. They wear Pakistani clothes at home and when they go to the Masjid .... it is important for me that they carry on with our religion. As you know most Pakistanis send their 'deads' to be buried in their village grave with proper prayer. This is all part of our religion.

## Separate Schools

Some sections of the Muslim communities in Britain have been strong supporters of separate voluntary schools (Islamia, 1992). Such schools are meant to be established along the same lines as those of various Christian denominations, e.g. Roman Catholics. The recent High Court decision (*Times Educational Supplement*, 20th May 1992) upholding the rights of Muslim parents in Islington is encouraging to those citizens who believe in equity and fairness. A Muslim manual worker (Birmingham) commented:

We need separate schools to educate our youngsters according to the Koranic principles, especially girls. Girls should cover their bodies and always appear modest in public — no make-up, hair-dos or jewellery. Learn to recite the Koran. In comprehensive schools they pick up the bad habits of white girls ... we can't tolerate this.

There was no enthusiasm among our Hindu and Sikh parents for separate schools along religious lines. The following were typical responses: A Sikh engineer (Birmingham):

> What is the point? We have to live in this country ... learn their ways, habits, manners, language to get jobs. I say it would be a backward step leading to segregation.

A Hindu shopkeeper (Birmingham) endorsed this:

> I am against this; I know some Muslims favour setting up of such schools. But their religion is very strict. In our religion women have equality or even more than equality. My sons have done very well in grammar schools ... we have taught them our religion.

In Vancouver there is already one Khalsa high school for the Sikh children. According to the principal of the school:

> Sikh boys and girls need such a school to build their positive religious identities along with good academic achievements. Boys and girls need to develop brother and sister-like relationships rather than emphasise their sexuality. They learn 'Shabid Keertan' and recitation of the Guru Granth Sahib. We feel this is the way to build their strong positive identity to live in a dominant white Christian society. We teach obviously Punjabi as well as Sikh literature.

However like the Hindu and Sikh parents in the UK, with one exception, the respondents in Vancouver showed no interest in separate schools. Typical replies were as follows. A Sikh journalist (Vancouver):

> This is not going to be good for our community. It will lead to self-segregation. Schools are secular here. We can teach them our religion at home and Gurudwaras.

An Hindu stall owner (Vancouver):

> I believe in tolerance and mutual respect. These come better in a multicultural situation. Our kinds have to mix with others eventually. Why not from the very beginning? I am totally opposed to them. Anyway these schools would find it difficult to have properly qualified Sikh/Hindu teachers. They have to employ teachers from other communities. I see it as a waste of time and anti multicultural.

## Parents' Participation

This is one of the problematic areas for the Asian parents. They tend to think (no doubt based on their personal experience in India and elsewhere) that 'education' is mainly the concern of teachers, and that parents should not meddle with their childrens' schooling. Such an attitude is, to a degree, also prevalent among the educated middle classes (Ghuman, 1980b). A Sikh office worker (Vancouver) explained:

> I only go when there is a meeting of parent–teacher association ... maybe I should get involved. (What about your wife?) My wife works, but she is even less involved. She is not comfortable with her language; this is the major cause.

A large majority of Asian parents do not have sufficient command of English to talk to teachers. Some do not show interest in an overt manner. A mill worker (Vancouver) was candid about his lack of interest:

> I was ashamed ... he (his son) invited me to go and see him play basketball; I did not. Then he won the individual prize for his play. Another time he asked me to drop him at a tournament; I reluctantly did. Later on our neighbour came rushing in saying congratulations, your son has won a trophy, the best sharp shooter. I felt stupid about it. But now I give him full support ... bought him a full gear.

The evaluation report on the Vancouver School Board's race relations policy (Fisher & Echols, 1989: 62) makes similar points: some of the reasons given for non-involvement are: language barrier; long hours of work and their traditional attitude 'not to show disrespect to the teachers' as teachers are considered to have high status and perceived to be fully competent to deal with educational problems. However, a housewife (Vancouver) related a very interesting encounter with the schools:

> I used to help my daughter with her arithmetic at home; taught her counting by using fingers. I was called in by the head. He was angry and said: 'don't confuse your child by teaching in an Indian way'. He made the same remark when I started teaching Punjabi at home. So I haven't helped her since.

This may be an isolated example, but it does reveal a lack of sensitivity on the part of some teachers who are too ethno-centric to see any thing of interest in other cultures, and so may unwittingly put students off their home values and beliefs.

There were some parents who showed positive and active interest in their youngsters' education. A Hindu manual worker (Birmingham) enthused:

> I see that he does his homework ... I can't help him but give up support by staying around. Making sure TV is not on. Because of our interest,

teachers have started giving homework regularly.

A Sikh mill worker (Vancouver) had a different angle on the problem:

> Most parents want good progress of their children at school ... of course a lot depends on the family and varies from one to another. Also depends on the children; they can stimulate interest in parents.

Overall my impression is that most parents in our sample, both in Birmingham and Vancouver, had high expectations of their youngsters, but were not sure how best to help them. They are happy to provide facilities, expenses and encouragement, but feel less confident about getting involved in the activities of such bodies as parents' associations or governing bodies of schools.

In Vancouver our formal and informal discussions with home–school workers indicate that most parents did not attend formal meetings owing to the language difficulty but the situation has improved, and continues to improve, since translation and interpretation facilities have been introduced. Clearly here is an important issue on which both the community leaders and the schools, through the home–school workers, should concentrate to secure better parental involvement.

## Parents' Views of Teachers and General Satisfaction With the Education System

Overall, parents were very pleased with the teachers' sound professionalism. A number paid compliments to the teachers' integrity and the hard work they put in to help their children. Farm owner and wife (Vancouver):

> Teachers explain everything — Canadian system is good. Choice is there. Those who don't want to study, teachers ignore them though!

Lab technician (Vancouver):

> My kids had no problems with teachers — others had, not with teachers though — there was a case of a boy who wore a turban. He was harassed by the kids. Teachers helped him and he also stood for himself.

Farm worker (Vancouver):

> Yes, I am very pleased with the education. My eldest is doing medicine. The other one got scholarship at grade 12. All my girls are at honours list ... I am very proud of my children. They are under my wing and influence.

Likewise, responses of parents from the Birmingham area were positive. A

Muslim restaurant owner (Birmingham) narrated:

> My children are benefiting from education; teachers are good. When I go on parents' day, they say nice things about my children. They are making good progress, I have no complaints.

However, a few parents from Birmingham (4/24) expressed some disquiet. A Sikh chemist (Birmingham) recounted the following disturbing event:

> I am fairly pleased; but this headmaster unfortunately gave me wrong advice about my son. Bhupnider, when fifteen, was told to leave school and work in a factory. Headmaster said: 'He will fix him in a job'. I did not agree I sent him to a college of further education. If I hadn't taken interest he would not have become a pharmacist.

An Hindu mini-market owner (Birmingham) also had a similar problem:

> There was Mr — as head. He said my eldest son won't do well at 11+ exams (he is not made of that fibre ... was his exact remark). The headmaster had a reputation for being prejudiced. I thought teacher shouldn't be. I said to my wife: 'teachers' opinions are not generally wrong'. So my wife said: 'He may be biased, I don't believe him'. We used all our resources to help him ... he passed his 11+ exams and went to a grammar school and then to a university.

The parents in Vancouver, however, were far more enthusiastic. A Sikh mill worker (Vancouver) expressed it well:

> Teachers are really dedicated; my teacher in further education marks 90 pieces of work every week and gives us back with comments. In India you never get them back. There is a good commitment of teachers: give you handouts and use visual aids and modern teaching technologies. Same is true of children's school.

## Social Issues

### Equality of boys and girls

The majority of parents (30/50) said that they believed in giving equal opportunity to girls, putting them on a par with boys. On further questioning, however, it became clear that what they meant was educational opportunity rather than the general 'freedom' enjoyed by boys. This observation is in accord with the comments of boys and girls both in Birmingham and Vancouver. A Sikh machine turner and his nurse wife (Vancouver) elaborated:

In our family we don't treat boys and girls differently. That is the basic point of the Sikh religion: woman is equal to man. This is the teaching of Guru Nanak. Some parents don't do that, their ethics and morals are different.

A Sikh farm owner and his wife (Vancouver) were also candid:

Yes, absolutely. (Even going out?) I don't mean that, I mean for studies and education. My daughter has become a legal secretary, now she is studying to be a teacher.

An unemployed Muslim worker (Birmingham) expressed a similar view:

The Koran says in education, girls should have the same rights as boys. My daughter can study as much she likes, but I have to protect her more than my boys from other bad influences ... Though I know some very traditional backward Muslim parents who want to withdraw their daughters at the earliest possible and have them married.

Asian parents are very protective of their daughters because of their perceptions of the host society's problems with drugs and undue emphasis on sex. A home–school worker (Vancouver) made an important point:

In Vancouver schools they are putting condom machines, this has really frightened a lot of parents. Parents are scared to send their girls to school dances, because of drugs and promiscuous sex ... I feel I would have done the same, if I were not in the school system. Parents' fears are quite genuine.

The Sikh and Hindu parents tended to be more liberal in their attitudes towards girls. A Sikh trade union official (Vancouver) gave a thoughtful reply:

This is a major concern ... even in Punjab it is the case, if a girl acquires a boyfriend, it is a matter of disgrace and dishonour. We have to work on this one and learn to compromise; find a middle way ... bend a little. I have very good relations with my children, though. I keep the dialogue going.

I did not find it prudent to probe further on the issue of dating (going out). From their other comments it was obvious that most of them disapprove of such European customs and would not like school staff and others to encourage it. However, from my observations and informal contacts, it became clear that a lot of parents turn a blind eye if their son dates a white girl. Apparently they hope that it is a temporary relationship — a passing phase. But this is a major source of resentment and grievance of Asian (Indo-Canadian) girls. Comments such as: 'Why boys?' or 'It isn't fair' are frequently heard in Asian homes.

There are no simple ways out of this dilemma, except to hope for a compromise solutions to emerge. A Sikh mother, who works as a civil servant (Birmingham) explained:

> I say to my son, if you meet a girl you like, ask her home and we would discuss matters. (Any girl?) I would prefer a Punjabi Sikh, followed by a Hindu and then perhaps a white or a Muslim.

The Chinese community in Vancouver allows and even tacitly encourages teenagers dating amongst their own community. I was told by an experienced Asian woman teacher that such a practice is to be found in the Hounslow Indian community. Drury (1991), researching in Nottingham with Sikh girls, found that they were facing a lot of difficulties with regard to boyfriends and attending disco parties. She found 26% of the girls believed in breakaway non-conformity on this issue, which indicates the potency of this issue among young adolescents. Clearly there is a wide gulf between parents' expectation and young people's ambitions.

## Arranged marriages

This is one of the most difficult and painful issues which the community faces in Canada and Britain. By tradition, marriages are arranged by parents and go-betweens, mainly on caste, religion and social class considerations. The opinions and feelings of youngsters were rarely taken into account. However, this custom has changed somewhat, and is changing in India and Pakistan, especially amongst the educated middle classes. Parents in Canada and the UK are also trying to modify this rigid custom by allowing a degree of choice and a limited chaperoned courtship.

But there is a significant number of parents who are from the village background, and are steeply immersed in their past traditions. A graphic account of this is given by a Sikh journalist (Vancouver):

> A lot of problems, cultural problems, our values are feudal ... marriage problems. A girl was murdered and burnt only three days ago. This is still happening. Kids are mentally tortured, they are compelled to marry.

Some parents feel under obligation to their kinsfolk in India and Pakistan and would like to help them by arranging for their boys/girls' entry to Canada and the UK through an arranged marriage. But such marriages are on the decline as the resentment of second-generation youngsters is growing. A Hindu mill worker (Vancouver) observed:

Forced arranged marriages don't work. I have seen 8 or 9 cases since 1970. These educated girls won't accept boys from India. There are some cases of suicide. This is our community's weakness, it shouldn't happen like this.

An unemployed Muslim worker (Birmingham) also expressed his puzzlement:

In our community marriages are arranged within the extended family network ... usually cousins. Boys from Pakistan are sometimes uneducated and they can't cope with girls from there. It doesn't work. It creates a lot of friction and problems in the family. Some people are beginning to understand this. ..... We should not oppress and consider young peoples' feelings. My eldest son agreed to his marriage; that is within the family.

Most parents (40/50) were of the view that this custom has to change to accommodate to the new situation. A Hindu clerical worker (Birmingham) explained:

I was rigid with my eldest son. He has revolted and gone for the English way. With my younger son I am flexible. For instance he knows a few girls; one day he is going to bring one home. I will certainly look into the matter ... if he insists (for marriage) he would have my blessings.

Similar sentiments were expressed by parents in Vancouver, as the following extracts demonstrate:

I tell her (niece), find a boy and let us know, we will fix it ... teachers tend to encourage kids to be Westernised, not openly but through school dances and other activities.

They can't be that rigid, they (parents) have to give something. It is happening. I have seen daughter meet a boy, they know each other. OK. They let them marry. So there are some moves ... some don't simply because of tradition.

The pattern which emerges from our interview is an interesting one: most Hindu and Sikh parents, both in Birmingham and Vancouver, show signs of flexibility and have already accepted a limited form of dating and are now modifying arranged marriage practices to meet the needs of their young boys and girls. The Muslim parents (6/8), however, are still quite traditional and would like the old custom of marriage within the extended family to continue.

## Equality of opportunity and racism

All the parents from Birmingham thought that their sons and daughters would not enjoy equality of opportunity with the whites. This observation is based on their personal experience, as a Hindu office worker (Birmingham) explained:

> No I don't think so. Racism is the basic cause. It will always be there. I have lived in this country for 25 years and gone through the process and I have met it; he will too. The majority will feel very alienated. There may be further unrest. They won't accept it; they will fight for it. Their thinking is very close to the British, they would demand their rights.

A lapsed Sikh accountant and his wife (Birmingham) explained:

> This fact we have to accept — never be treated as the whites. Kids have to be twice as good ... nearly twice. I say it to my son, you have to outshine the whites. When I came to this country my degree was not accepted, I had to start all over again. It is alright now; I am a qualified accountant, despite all the difficulties.

The Canadian parents were slightly more positive; only about half the parents thought their youngster would not be treated on a par with the whites. A Hindu office worker (Vancouver) commented:

> I think so, but there is always a concern ... depends a lot on the Government policy, it has a role to play. It can play a negative role. Also depends on what type and how long they have been in power. The English politics had a lot of influence here ... we have gone backwards on the issue.

A Sikh stall owner and his wife (Vancouver) were rather philosophical:

> Depends how good you are. In society nobody gives you, you have to take it. There are some discriminations everywhere. Even we do it to others ... look at the Biharis in Punjab. That's part of the nature's cycle. If 95% of the system is OK, it is good. We do it to the Chamars (low castes) .... should look at our own community.

On the whole, parents in Vancouver seem to be more optimistic about their youngsters' future than in the UK, where the degree of prejudice and discrimination in employment, housing and other walks of life has not changed since 1963, according to the researches of the Policy Studies Institute (Brown, 1984). Parents in Canada tend to believe in the North American dream 'hard work and perseverance will get you there eventually, despite the odds'.

## Identity of youngsters

*Who am I?*

This is one of the most important questions facing both the parents and the second-generation youngsters. The responses of the Birmingham parents are quite different from those of the parents in Vancouver. The Birmingham sample was quite realistic in perceiving their childrens' identity rooted in their own culture. A Hindu shopkeeper (Birmingham) reflected:

> This is a tough one. I would like to hope they would be considered as British Hindus. Though my son considers himself as an English boy: 99% of his friends are English, except his two cousins. But recently he has got interested in Bhangra music. Also he has been staying up to watch Kabadi (an Indian field game) quite late.

A Muslim factory worker (Birmingham) gave a straightforward answer:

> My kids are Muslims and Pakistanis. (Aren't they British?) Yes, they were born in Birmingham. But I have brought them up in the Muslim way: they can speak Punjabi and Urdu, read the Koran, observe Ramadan; wear Punjabi clothes at home and also listen to Pakistani songs.

A Sikh chemist (Birmingham) thought his children have bicultural identities:

> I suppose they have both — Punjabi and English. They can read the holy books, understand Sikhism and our customs. At the same time, they attend English schools, speak English, watch TV, and have English friends.

Another Sikh shopkeeper (Birmingham) was very cautious:

> My sons won't be fully accepted ... I doubt it. We would be always Indian. My son says: he is English, I say no you are not English. You are English by place of birth. You don't become that person by living in the country. But look at the Jews; they remained Jews — never became German. I would say first Indian and then British. Whatever happens, if you line them up their colour stands up. If you tell them they are British, you would be leading them wrong; they won't have the same privileges as the white British, in jobs and everything.

In contrast, the Vancouver parents were far more sure of their children's identities. A Sikh journalist (Vancouver) reasoned:

> Full Canadian (pause) I think so. They (his children) are certain. I have never thought about it, even now I don't feel Canadian, Canada is my country. Frankly I am mentally in Punjab. I ran Punjabi newspaper. I thought in Punjabi, wrote in Punjabi and joked in Punjabi. But they do it in English. They are much committed; they won't go back.

A skilled Sikh worker (Vancouver) made a very perceptive observation:

> Yes, they would feel Canadians and should be treated as such. We can be

good Sikhs/Hindus and good Canadians ..... but sometimes I see problems. We are called visible people. We have to try harder than the average Jo. I say to my children you get the *best of both worlds*; but if you give up your home customs; they won't *fully* accept you. Like other kids call my children East Indians; though they were born here, with no accents. For them colour and turban become important.

The parents showed more enthusiasm about a bright future for themselves and their children. A Sikh store owner and his wife (Vancouver) captured the essence of high hopes:

My son is yet too young to be aware. I like to collect good things from every culture and make this world more beautiful ..... make it more complete. There is beauty in every culture. I will encourage our son to be multicultural: a world citizen and a good Canadian.

## Friendship

It was considered important to know the parents' views on their youngsters' friends. On this topic there was little difference between the two samples; the parents approved of their sons' and daughters' friends and spoke enthusiastically of inter-ethnic friendships. A Sikh nurse (Vancouver):

Our kids have friends of all groups, but more Chinese friends really. My daughter had a Cantonese friend for four years and she also learnt to speak Cantonese.'

A trade union official summed up the spirit of the group with this cryptic remark:

No matter to me, children are children and race or colour doesn't come into it. I accept their choice.

As described earlier in Chapter 2, the Vancouver schools are truly multicultural in that there is a mix of 1/3 whites, 1/3 Chinese and 1/3 Indo-Canadians. However, the situation in Birmingham is different. The schools chosen for study are over 95% Asian; therefore friendship from the other ethnic groups is rather restricted. But the parents showed a very liberal attitude towards acceptance of their adolescents' friends from amongst all ethnic groups.

A Muslim clerical worker (Birmingham) painted this picture:

His friends are West Indians. He has white friends and some Indians. My daughters' friends are Indian girls. My son does not bring girls home; I

might have hesitation in accepting that. I welcome them all. I like it ... that
my children have friends from different cultures.

Another Muslim factory worker (Birmingham) had this to say:

Friends are mixed ... all groups. They don't come home, they go to the
Park etc. With the whites, they talk a lot with each other, but don't bring
them home.

From my own observation of the two schools in Vancouver where I spent
two weeks, it became clear that there was a good inter-ethnic mixing and com-
panionship. The enthusiastic way in which both teacher and students described
their inter-ethnic friendships is evident from the preceding chapters.


## Dress and Food

Outwardly the two items are important markers of ethnic distinction. Dress
is much more important than food, especially in relation to Asian women and
young girls. The majority of parents (42/50) either were willing or resigned to
accept that their young sons and daughters are going to wear European styles of
clothing. A Sikh mill worker and his wife (Vancouver) elaborated:

They wear our clothes at home or on special social or religious functions.
For office they wear like the other Canadians. Children would be left out if
they wore Punjabi clothes at school and at office. Older generation (i.e.
people who were in Canada by the turn of the century) were simple folks
from the villages and stuck to their customs rigidly. We are changing for
the sake of our kids ... say my daughter goes to school wearing a Punjabi
suit (Salwar & Kameez), she would look like and stick out as a cartoon. We
don't want that.

It was emphasised by most parents that they are willing to go along with
their sons' and daughters' choice of clothes as long as they are in good taste.
They were particularly concerned that their daughters should not pick up the so
called 'bad habits' of dressing in short skirts or low-cut blouses. The key word
often used was 'modesty'. A Hindu clerical worker (Birmingham) expressed it
well:

We are very liberal about dress and their fashion clothes. But we must draw
a line somewhere. I don't want to see my daughter look like some of
Gora's (white) girl; all made up and cheap.

However, there was a minority (8/50) of parents who were rather orthodox in
their views. A Muslim factory worker (Birmingham) explained:

Our religion is very clear on this ... girls must cover their bodies and should not in any way dress provocatively. Schools in Birmingham have been very good about it. Girls can wear scarves over their heads and can wear Pakistani trousers rather than skirts in schools. (What about boys?) We are less strict on them, they are not in danger of moral corruption.

The rigid stand of some parents on this issue has caused difficulties for their daughters. A small minority of them resort to surreptitious methods of dressing as described by a social worker:

They keep a lot of spare clothes in their school lockers and change when they come to school and back again when they go home.

As regards food, numerous changes have been made by the majority of parents (46/50). All sorts of mixed food is prepared and bought for consumption. These changes have been made mainly in response to their young people's demand for variety and convenience. The traditional breakfast of 'paratha' (highly buttered chappati) and yoghurt has been replaced by cereals and toast, except on an occasional weekend. Lunch is often taken at a workplace with a mixture of indigenous and English food.

The evening meal is the only meal which is along traditional lines — chappatis, lentil, vegetable/meat curries and salads. Religious strictures are observed by most Muslim parents and all Hindus except two who are vegetarians.


## General Comments and Conclusions

The parents in Birmingham as well as in Vancouver expressed their general satisfaction with the schooling which their youngsters were going through. This is in line with previous research findings in the field (Knight, 1988; Smith & Tomlinson, 1989). But differences in opinion between the two groups of parents emerged over a range of specific social and educational issues. The parents in Vancouver thought that their youngsters are treated very fairly by the schools. This is supported by evidence produced by a research team which investigated the race relations policy of the Vancouver School Board (Fisher & Echols, 1989). Over 85% (out of a total sample of 135) Indo-Canadian parents felt that the identity of their children is respected by schools; only 15% were unsure or disagreed. The quality of race relations in schools, as seen by the Indo-Canadian parents, rated (5.27) on a seven-point scale, which is nearly as high as the mean of the whole sample of parents (5.46). My own observations confirms such a positive attitude amongst parents. They perceive the identities of their sons and daughters to be bicultural or even rooted in the Canadian culture. Further, parents believe that they will enjoy almost the same privileges and rights as their youngsters' white peers. Canada is seen by them as a land of golden opportunity where hard work, industriousness and qualifications are rewarded quite fairly. Such positive attitudes are based on their personal observations and experiences. Most of them came to Canada with very little, and now through persistent hard work, thrift and sheer doggedness have bought spacious houses, big cars and have been able to sponsor their relatives from their former home countries. A casual acquaintance remarked:

> For me this country is heaven. I live in a clear beautiful city, there are plenty of things to eat, there is a welfare system, a good education for my children and no hassle from the 'babus' (clerks) of civil service. If there is another heaven up above I don't know; but this is a real one for me.

Unemployment amongst the community is very low. Wives get employment as well, though these are often low-paid office cleaning jobs. On the negative side it was pointed out by the home–school workers, and confirmed by my own observations, that the community has become very materialistic and money-minded. The success of a family is measured in terms of its material possessions rather than by educational and cultural standards. The race for material improvement sometimes results in the needs of children and young people being overlooked. A saying in the community sums it up: 'Earned a lot of money, but lost a lot of our kids'.

The Birmingham parents, on the whole, were less sure of their young peoples' identity. They tended to think that, because British society does not fully accept their youngsters, their identities would mainly be rooted in their home cultures, even though for successful living, parents thought their offspring have to acquire elements of English culture.

The Muslim parents are keener and more organised in passing on the culture of the family as compared to the Hindus and Sikhs. Also, with the recent increase in negative, even hostile, media coverage of the Muslim attitude to the Gulf war and the Rushdie affair, the Muslim young people have tended to turn inwards. The Muslim youth, in the Midlands and elsewhere in Britain, have been known to give up snooker, beer and coke and to flood to the mosques for support and solidarity (confirmed by personal communications with local teachers). There is an increasing demand for new mosques in Birmingham, where there are already some 500 small and large institutions. Hindu families, according to my personal observations in the field, tend to be more liberal in their outlook. In most Hindu families, women often enjoy equal rights with men. Grandmothers and older women are even 'deified' — witness the new cult figure of the late Mrs Indira Ghandi, who became 'Mother India'. Hindu families are more willing to encourage and accept bicultural identities of their youngsters and to treat girls on a par with boys. The Sikh community falls somewhere between the Hindus and the Muslims.

My impressions were that parents in non-manual jobs were not at ease with their situation, especially in England. This is based on their personal experiences and observations. Several of them had very high expectations, prior to migrating, but their qualifications and experiences were not always recognised. Most of them had to gain extra qualifications to obtain jobs which formerly they were doing in India and Pakistan. Several had faced discrimination and racism from their employers and colleagues. However, parents without professional qualifications were more content. They have realised their ambitions beyond their wildest dreams. They have bought houses, owned cars, have sent money home, and have generally raised their standard of living enormously.

From my own observations and experience of Asian communities it seems that well-off middle-class Hindu, Sikh and Muslim families are increasingly sending their children to fee-paying public schools. The thinking behind this trend is that young people need the best of English/Canadian education to compete for jobs with the whites. Young people would come out from such schools with 'proper accents', good command of English and sound academic qualifications. They are not too concerned about the retention of their mother-tongue or other aspects of their culture being encouraged by schools. They feel they can deal with those aspects of education.

Bhachu (1985c: 15), a well-established anthropologist from a Punjabi background, summarised her research findings in the area as follows:

> In interviewing parents, I found that their most striking expectation (which applies in every case, whether it be Muslim, Sikh or a Hindu, Punjabi or Guejerati etc.) is that their children should get at least 'O' and 'A' levels; also, they should go in for further education of some type. For boys a university place is a must …. for girls, the main concern is that they should go in for further education locally ….. they know of strategies to improve the educational chances of their children or rather they feel that a private education will guarantee a certain degree of upward mobility.

A long-serving headmaster of a largely Asian school carried out a piece of research on the needs, wants and aspirations of his students' parents (Knight, 1988). His findings are broadly in accord with my findings on Asian parents. He writes:

> Above all parents want a good standard of education for their children. The chief criteria by which they assess quality are:

(a)   the achievement of good external examination results;
(b)   a rigorous approach to study, focusing for the most part on key sub-
      ject areas;
(c)   a consistent, strong and authoritative approach to discipline.

The Asian communities are making changes in the arranged marriage customs. They are now less likely to follow the rigidity of old traditions. A lot
depends of course on the sort of background they have come from: for instance
rural background communities are slow in adapting to the new situations, whereas those from urban middle-classes are more flexible and open. Other
researchers in Canada and the US. have found a similar trend. Vaidyanthan &
Naidoo (1991:48) summarise their research findings as follows.

Overall, 'with regard to contemporary marriage in the Asian Indian community in Canada', two major trends can be identified: (1) more flexibility
in parental authority in the host country as compared to the ancestral country, and (2) an increase in the independence and decision making power of
the second generation. This particular sample of Asian Indians exhibit
adoptive behaviour, having discovered that an attitude of compromise and
balance is required for optimal functioning within the host context.

# 5 Response of Asian Communities

I think Yes, they would be accepted as Canadians but not as white Canadians. There would be some people who think if the colour is right, then only they are real Canadians. Some still say: 'Why don't you go back'. But I say to our youngsters: you get the best of both worlds and ignore the ignorant people. Keep good things of your culture — language, religion, respect for elders, sense of history etc. But if you give up your home customs, they won't fully accept you. (Sikh president of a Gurudwara, Vancouver)

As described in Chapter 1, the immigrants from the Indian sub-continent came from a variety of religious, caste, social and regional backgrounds. Their settlement patterns in the UK and Canada also reflected this situation. For instance, Sikhs from the Punjab are to be found in large numbers in Handsworth, Smethwick, Wolverhampton and the English Midlands, and in Vancouver, Surrey and Abbotsford in British Columbia.

The main basis of community organisations is religion. There are local Sikh bodies, Muslim organisations and Hindu 'Sabhas' all formed around the places of worship.

The response of Asian communities to adolescents' needs and concerns varies from community to community as there is little inter-religious dialogue or concerted effort. A number of community leaders were interviewed to ascertain their opinions on a range of educational and social issues. The details are in Table 5.1.

**Table 5.1.** Community leaders' sample

|         | Vancouver | Birmingham |
|---------|-----------|------------|
| Sikhs   | 3         | 2          |
| Hindus  | 2         | 2          |
| Muslims | —         | 2          |
|         | 5         | 6  =11     |

All the persons selected for interviews had a significant position within the community: for example, one was president of a Gurudwara or Mandir, one a representative on the Commission for Racial Equality and one a school governor. They have been in the UK and Canada for over 20 years and their average age is around 50 years. They know their respective communities from within and were willing to talk to me on the understanding that my work would, hopefully, lead to a better appreciation of parental concerns on educational and social matters. Very informal semi-structured interviews were undertaken, mostly through Punjabi/Urdu, though English was also used intermittently. Therefore the responses quoted in the text reflect the translated extracts from Punjabi and Urdu and also verbatim English sentences.

## Religious Places of Worship

All leaders were of the opinion that their holy places are the focus of their communities' social and cultural activities. A Sikh (Vancouver) explained:

> We have now several Gurudwaras, they are the heart of the community. Wedding, family celebrations, funerals etc. are conducted by the Bhais. Local politics and Indian politics are discussed there. We have eminent Sikh leaders from India who come to preach and collect donations for various causes.

Similar sentiments were expressed by other leaders. The social roles of the holy places were greatly emphasised. A Hindu Justice of the Peace (Birmingham) elaborated:

> We have a room for the elderly attached to the temple. There is a TV and video and reading materials. There are facilities for tea making. Free meals are offered on Wednesday evenings.

The Muslim community in Birmingham is very well organised around several mosques, as there are theological (Suni/Shia) and regional (Bangladashi, Pakistani) differences. A Muslim (Birmingham) explained:

> You see it is Ramadan now. Most Muslims would be fasting, saying their prayers. Mosques are full ... there are altogether 500, including small ones. We are a very religious community and would like our children to learn and practice our religion. This is the heart of our community.

All the community leaders were of the opinion that it is one of the main responsibilities of religious places to teach children and young people the fundamentals of their respective religions. A Sikh from Vancouver explained:

Young people learn through example ... parents are urged to bring young people with them. We have books for kids, free meals and we are thinking of building a recreation centre as an attraction.

All the places of worship are used for the teaching of the mother-tongue on weekends, particularly on Sundays. A Hindu from Birmingham commented:

In Gita Mandir we teach Hindi on Saturdays and Sundays; attendance is not good, but it is getting better. We have a Pandit and women teachers from the community. Most of our books are from India ... there is an attempt to produce books in the country. It is slow but coming along.

All the leaders agreed that schools should include the teaching of community languages in the school curriculum as far as possible. They felt that this policy would give status to community languages. A Sikh president of Gurudwara (Vancouver) reasoned:

My kids learn French, I say why not Punjabi as well. Most parents who come to Gurudwara support this. I feel some teachers are just prejudiced and they make excuses to explain away why it can't be done.

In Birmingham, I was informed there are weekend community schools to teach maths and other school subjects. The idea is to supplement the school work in some subjects. A Muslim part-time teacher (Birmingham) explained:

In ... Majsid they teach a lot of school subjects. There is a small charge — but a lot comes from the Mosque funds. This is to give our kids a good start to pass school examinations.

# Educational Matters

There was a consensus of opinion on the importance of educational qualifications for the young people. But opinions differed on such matters as single-sex schools, separate voluntary-aided schools and the teaching of some subjects.

### Single-sex schools

The Muslim leaders (Birmingham) were of the opinion that single-sex schools at the secondary stage are important for the healthy growth of their young people.

According to our religion, girls and boys should be taught separately because this is a very vulnerable age. Also we think girls should concentrate on those skills which are important for running the home. They should dress modestly and should not learn such subjects as dance or drama, but should learn the basics of our religion.

However, the Hindus and Sikhs were less keen. They did not see it as a problem. A turbaned Sikh priest (Vancouver) explained:

No we don't mind ... our community is open on this. Even in India co-education is being accepted. Of course there are some very traditional parents who want separate schools. The majority would like to see good discipline in co-education schools though. Parents get scared when they hear of drugs and condom machines at schools.

**Separate schools**

Again the Muslim leaders were very keen on having voluntary-aided schools like the established Roman Catholics and the Methodists. But the Hindu and Sikh leaders were not enthusiastic. A Hindu leader (Birmingham) reasoned:

I don't think Hindus want it; our religion is accommodating. But I know a lot of Muslim parents want them. They know how to fight for their rights. They are very assertive. Islam is a very strict religion; it creates more problems for girls. In our community women have an upper hand. Their role is equally important.

A turbaned Sikh (Birmingham) rejected the idea of separate schools:

I don't agree with this (what about the community?) They don't mind ... you will never mix. It is not right. I think we should integrate with the whites. But I also know that a lot of the whites don't want to integrate with us. It is a problem, but this is no solution.

**Teaching of drama and music**

Muslim leaders were not in favour of teaching these subjects, especially drama classes where boys and girls mixed a lot, though drama is taught in one of the Birmingham schools chosen for the current research. For the Sikhs and Hindus the teaching of such subjects is quite acceptable, provided not too much time is spent on them. A Sikh (Vancouver) remarked:

Our community doesn't mind; but sometimes too much time is spent on such subjects and students have less time for other important subjects. When they leave schools they have to find jobs ... they are not in drama. The study of maths, English and science is very important.

### Parents' participation

Out of the eleven leaders, only one had not attended university back at home. Therefore they were well aware of the importance of the parents' role in education. But a turbaned Sikh, former army officer, (Vancouver) explained:

> 95% of parents are from the village background — they can't speak English. They also find it hard to face people in authority ... But once I went to parents' evening I was completely ignored by the teachers, because I had a turban on and they thought I won't be able to speak English. Things are getting better though, with home–school workers.

A Sikh president of a Gurudwara (Vancouver) commented:

> Our parents don't go to school generally watch TV or drink at home. They have very little contact with teachers. I think parents' involvement is a must ... one of the most important. I think parents have more influence as compared to teachers, school boards or the government.

This lack of active participation in young people's education was attributed to poor knowledge of English, lack of confidence and experience and in some cases too much attention being paid to making money.

## Social Issues

The respondents dealt with the important issues which the young people face; namely, dating, arranged marriages, identity, equality of opportunity and racism. On the whole, their opinions are close to the views of the parents discussed in Chapter 4. But they tend to emphasise different points depending on their religious beliefs.

### Dating and arranged marriages

All the interviewees were of the opinion that dating is so alien to their established customs and practices that it will not be acceptable to the communities. A Sikh trade unionist (Vancouver) explained:

> No, Asian communities presently won't accept it ... may be gradually, next generation (third) when these young people grow up, even then perhaps within their own religious groups.

On arranged marriages, both the Hindu and Sikh leaders gave similar responses. A Hindu store-owner (Birmingham) explained:

> There are two types: one from India and the other from this country. The one from India are proving highly unsuccessful ... boys and girls had hard times. 35-40% were satisfied, and 20% ended in divorce. In this country, boys and girls meet, there is a limited dating, often without the parents' knowledge. I think more and more marriages would be along this pattern.

The Muslim leaders were also resigned to accepting this situation, but were hopeful that parents would have more say in match-making. A Muslim, governor of a school (Birmingham), argued:

> Parents realise that sponsoring boys and girls from Pakistan doesn't work. The important thing is to have the full consent of young people before marriage, otherwise it is difficult. In some cases our young men have white girl- friends; our parents turn a blind eye. But parents should be fully aware of the situation, otherwise they would be storing trouble for themselves.

### Identity of young people and biculturalism

All the interviewees from Birmingham were unanimous on the question of 'acceptance' of young people by the whites. None of them thought they would be fully accepted by British society. A Sikh part-time teacher of handicapped children (Birmingham) explained:

> Some second-generation became too anglicised ... they move away from Punjabi culture. They came back to the fold when the National Front and Skin-heads started attacking them physically. They were not accepted by the mainstream either.

A Sikh teacher, also a school governor (Birmingham), was very negative:

> They are even called second-generation immigrants, though they were born in this country. Of course there are terrible name calling as well as you know — Paki. Even most educated people call them Indian or Pakistani, sometimes they add origins. But it reflects the deep held attitudes. They would never be accepted freely ... second-class citizens at best.

However a Hindu school governor (Birmingham) was a little more optimistic:

> They are becoming bicultural ... learning the ways of both communities. Sometimes I feel sorry for them. What happens when they come and face racism? Schools can play a part. It is high time they accept full responsibility. The colour of skin should be not a determining factor. Society has to change ... We are here to stay.

All the respondents from Birmingham thought that the identities of young people would primarily be rooted in their own home culture, though they would also learn social skills and gain qualifications from the British society.

However, the Canadian leaders were confident that, though somewhat handicapped by their colour, they will be accepted as Indo-Canadians. A Sikh president of a Gurudwara reasoned:

> I think 'Yes' as Canadians, but not as white Canadians. There would be some people who think if the colour is right, then only they are Canadians. Some still say: 'Why don't you go back'. But I say to our youngsters: 'You get the best of both worlds, and ignore the ignorant people'. Keep good things of your own culture ...... language, religion, respect for elders, sense of history etc. But if you give up your home customs, they won't fully accept you.

For the Canadian community leaders the concern was that their young people may become too Canadian and give up all aspects of the home culture. A Sikh writer (Vancouver) argued:

> Some of our values are medieval, quite out of date. Young people are rejecting these. But then it becomes a general revolt against parents ... rejecting language, religion, literature, the whole lot. Our community and parents have to change and accept new ways of marriage and freedom for the young.

## Specific needs of young people

All the respondents were asked what their community were doing to cater for the special needs of young people. The importance of such a question was not fully appreciated by every interviewee; for them such special needs either do not exist or are a figment of young peoples' imagination. A Muslim restaurant owner (Birmingham) explained:

> I don't understand, they have plenty to eat, there is TV at home and at school they can learn a play. What else do they need?

I did not feel inclined to mention such matters as freedom for boys and girls to go out, choose their own clothes, play sports, and generally do things which young white people do. I thought such remarks would immediately be construed as antagonistic to their culture and might bring the interview to a premature end. However, there was a more perceptive response from a Sikh school governor:

> For our young people there are no clubs or youth clubs ... they are non-existent. Some kids are barred in the evenings from going out. Some run away to Bhangra or day-time Bhangra shows; give a dodge to the parents. Some of them are trapped by quite sinister people ... making money through drugs. There are pimps as well. Our communities' response is that they sit, talk and criticise in Temples, Masjids and Gurudwaras. Rarely we find someone with constructive suggestions. The only response is .... weekend and supplementary schools for religious instructions and the mother-tongue teaching. Young people need and want more.

Part of the difficulty is that most Asian parents did not experience much difficulty in their teenage years. There was a relatively smooth transition from childhood to adulthood, with adolescence only a minor episode in their lives. In most cases, revolts and discussions were easily resolved through the extended family network. Open breaches were few, as in practice the traditional customs and practices were largely accepted without question. A Punjabi Sikh part-time teacher (Birmingham) tries to unravel some of the problems:

> Our community hasn't responded ... these second-generation kids are demanding freedom. Some parents are changing on the marriage issue ... boys and girls can meet a number of times before saying yes or no. As regards youth clubs etc. ... I must say Gurudwaras haven't thought along these lines. But our community is strict with girls; they won't allow them the same freedoms as they would allow boys. Muslims are even stricter and very rigid, Hindus are more lenient.

A Hindu leader (Birmingham) was quite cynical about Sikh, Hindu and Muslim communities:

> Our parents were not educated (first generation) ... a lot of them are from the village background. Young people of second-generation are fluent in English and know the ways of the host society. In such cases they become the 'bosses' in the family ... explaining, translating for their parents and so on. There is a big gap between the parents and the kids. Parents, especially fathers, who can't even talk to their grown up kids. If there were youth clubs, there would be fights, because we believe in old ethics. Oh

my sister is dancing with that man! Only 10% are educated, and they would make changes. But others are only for religion and old values.

## General Comments and Conclusions

Communities' efforts have been mainly to provide support and help to the first-generation immigrants through the transference of institutions of 'home' societies: places of worship, community centres to cater for the needs of the elderly, networks of kith and kin relationships (Biradri/Bhaichara), grocery and video-cassette shops, etc. are some of the examples of such initiatives.

Asian communities have paid little attention to catering for the needs of young people. In a nationwide large-scale survey of Asian parents and young people CRE reported (Anwar, 1978), that nearly half the sample thought that the Asian community does not recognise and provide for the needs of youngsters.

As a summary the author (Anwar, 1978: 49) conclude: 'Generally Asians offer basic welfare services, accommodation, jobs, lending money if the need arises, etc. through their close family network. But they are unable to cope with the more subtle problems faced by the community as a whole and by the young people in particular.

Evidence from our small sample supports such a situation both in Birmingham and Vancouver. My own visits to the places of worship and Sunday schools also confirms this finding. Asian communities have yet to fully appreciate the difficulties of their young people, particularly girls, exposed to differing and often conflicting cultural experiences. Facilities for sports, recreational activities and social events (in some cases separate for boys and girls) have to be provided to keep young people off the street, otherwise they might start to engage in anti-social activities. Recent riots and inter-ethnic conflict in Blackburn, England, between the youth of Indian and Pakistani origins should be a warning to the community leaders who were generally unaware of the simmering discontent of their young people (*The Guardian*, 24th July 1992). According to the social workers I talked to, there are 'serious problems caused by unemployment in Birmingham and elsewhere in Britain and increasingly significant numbers of youngsters are involved in drugs and car thefts'. A social worker of ethnic minority origin explained:

Asian communities are too busy with the old order of things ... Koran says this. These kids are facing different sorts of problems ... threat of unemployment, rigid restrictions of family, particularly on girls, drugs and so on. I find it quite frustrating ... community leaders would not take it on board.

But the parents say: why do they (our kids) go away from us? Sometime all they want is to talk about their problems ... Teachers and others should organise meetings, conferences etc. to educate parents about these matters, because parents carry on the same way. Even things have changed in India and Pakistan, I say: cultures change ... these kids are bicultural and parents have to wake up to this reality.

# 6 Conclusions: Emerging Bicultural Identities

Do you feel Canadian or Indo-Canadian?

> I don't know — I follow other religion. I try to go to Church, I try to fit in.
> I do my best — I still believe in my religion (i.e. Hindu), but I can fit in
> both religions ... (pause) you have to; I do. I was raised here, I was a baby.
> My parents tried to make a Hindi (sic) — but I mix with East Indians and
> white people. They (my parents) have accepted my biculturalism (A
> Hindu/girl from Vancouver).

The project described here was planned to understand, illuminate and probe
into the difficulties, anxieties and concerns of young people (13–16 years) growing up in two large cities: Birmingham, England and Vancouver, Canada. To
grasp fully the complexities of social and educational issues, a number of young
people, parents, community leaders, teachers and counsellors were interviewed.
In addition, an established acculturation scale (Chapter 1:26) and a questionnaire
on family background were given to the young people to broaden the data base.
My in-depth knowledge of Asian communities, gained through very long-stand-
ing personal and professional contact, has been an additional source of information to complement the data gained through more systematic procedures.

In reporting work of this type, it is probable that the writer's perceptions,
attitudes, views and indeed prejudices may influence both the substance and
style of research. Therefore, I consider it imperative to state my own views
explicitly so that the reader is aware of such predilections.

It is inevitable that young people of Asian origin, growing up in Britain,
Canada and the US, will pick up some of the norms, values, habits and customs
of the host society. Because of the radical differences in family structure, religion and general 'world views', there are likely to be tensions between Asian
parents and their young people, particularly during adolescence. But such tensions may not inevitably lead to conflicts, anxieties, open breaches and alienation. Young peoples' lives can become richer and fuller by becoming bilingual
and well-versed in the histories and traditions of two cultures, provided there is

active and constructive support from teachers, parents and community leaders. However, I believe much depends on the reaction of the host society and its institutions. If the judiciary, the police, the civil service and business, commercial and industrial employers are biased against Asians, and engage in discriminatory practices, then the process of integration will be slowed down, if not completely halted. Most young people in such situations would probably stay with, or revert back to, their original identities. Some might become alienated from both cultures as they see 'faults' on both sides and became marginal people in society. Some might internalise 'weaker' points of their own culture and live in shame (because they feel inferior) and guilt (because they dislike or reject their family values).

First-generation Asian immigrants from the Indian sub-continent left their homes primarily to improve their standards of living and to have access to 'good quality' English/Canadian education. The vast majority of Asian immigrants in Britain and Canada are from the middle to upper-middle strata of the indigenous societies they come from. Therefore, they are highly motivated, aspiring and very ambitious individuals who want to climb up the social ladder by improving their economic and educational standards. The intentions of very many Asians were to stay in Britain for a short period (5–7 years) and then to return home with their savings to improve their family's fortune. But with the passage of time, 'intentions' to return weakened and eventually very few went back to settle in their home countries. Anwar (1979) describes their predicament in the well-known book, The Myth of Return. However, after 1945, immigration to Canada from India and Pakistan was more for permanent settlement.

The settlement patterns of Asians, both in Britain and Canada, have been along the lines of religious, regional and caste affiliations. As a result, there have emerged 'ethnic enclaves'. Communities have re-created the primary institutions of their respective home societies. The foremost of such institutions are Biraderi (the extended family network), places of worship and community organisations which are often aligned to Mosques/Gurudwaras/temples. Their reception in Britain was mixed; they were welcomed by industry where there was a shortage of manpower, but met a cool, if not hostile, reception from neighbours and indigenous communities. Most first-generation migrants, both in Canada and Britain, were content to confine themselves to their own communities and had little interaction with the indigenous white people. Their aims were modest: to work hard and save as much as possible for the folks back home. Later on, most of them used their savings to buy a house and/or sponsor a relative to join them in their new country of domicile. Most retained their religion and family loyalties, spoke their mother-tongue, kept their food habits and maintained their original social customs and practices (Chapter 1:20).

They were, and are, secure in their personal and social identities: for instance they are Muslims from Pakistan or Sikhs from the Punjab. I discovered in my interviews that the former small land-holders in India and Pakistan, now employed mainly as unskilled or semi-skilled workers in Birmingham and Vancouver, were more contented with their situation as compared to the professional people.

The latter did meet with difficulties in having their qualifications recognised in Britain and Canada and have, initially at any rate, often worked in non-professional jobs. Some had acquired extra qualifications from the country of domicile to regain their former professional status. There are a large number of graduates who have not been able to find anything other than semi-skilled jobs, for example, bus drivers. I have met several Indian graduates in Vancouver and Surrey (British Columbia) who are working in saw mills or canneries or are driving taxis. Some are bitter because of their situation, but the majority have come to accept their position as the option of going back is, or never was, a realistic one because of the very high unemployment rate among graduates. However, some started their own small businesses and have become very successful.

As regards the cultural identity of the second generation, the situation is complex: they have been called 'the half-way generation' (Thompson, 1974); 'between two cultures' (Watson, 1979); 'British Asians' (Wade & Souter, 1991) and just 'Asians' by the majority of indigenous whites.

The findings from the acculturation scale, the background questionnaire and interviews with a number of young people (Chapter 2:70) threw up several insights which have a bearing on their life-styles and identity. The young people favour a degree of acculturation: they support inter-ethnic friendship, celebrate Christmas, they like European-style clothes, watch English films and listen to Western pop music. However, there was overwhelming support for the maintenance of the mother-tongue, respect for parents, retention of family names and for aspects of family religion — suggesting adherence to home cultural values. The girls showed a higher degree of acculturation as compared to the boys (Tables 2.12 and 2.13). From the interview data, it also became clear that the girls strongly favour equality with boys in educational opportunities and 'personal freedom'. This turns out to be one of the most intractable issues for parents and the community to deal with. I will return to it presently.

From the results of the acculturation scale, it was inferred that the Indo-Canadian boys and girls are more in favour of taking up the norms and patterns of behaviour of the host society as compared to the British Asians (Table 2.11). Both the Indo-Canadian and Birmingham samples approve of those items on the scale which relate to gender equality, inter-ethnic friendship and going to

English cinemas. But, in addition, Indo-Canadians tend to feel that 'boys and girls should go out with white Canadians', and that 'our women should wear European clothes'. The other striking acculturation difference is that the Indo-Canadian adolescents are less sure of retaining their original Indian 'first' and 'middle' names (Chapter 2:45). A casual examination of the class register showed many changes and additions to Indian names. Daijit Singh Gill is modi-fied to David Gill, for instance and Dharampal is just Paul. The Sikh middle names of 'Singh' and 'Kaur', for boys and girls respectively, are often omitted. Further, they were hostile to the items on 'arranged marriages' and 'our customs are best for us'. During the interview, they appeared to me very confident and sure of their biculturalism and looked and behaved as if they were treated with respect and accorded full rights by their schools. In contrast, the students from Birmingham were less sure of their ethnic identity and left me with a feeling that they were somewhat anxious about their future in England. Professor Bagley (Bagley, 1989:103), who has taught and researched both in Britain and Canada, writes:

> There is little evidence that the curriculum of the average secondary school in Britain has this. The results, especially for black students in Britain, is a degree of profound alienation which negates any concept of universality in education (Bagley, 1982). No systematic evidence exists of such profound alienation amongst the children of black and Asian immigrants to Canada.

The Indo-Canadian students and parents I interviewed did not think there was any prejudice or discrimination in schools. Furthermore, the majority of the students thought they would get equality of treatment with white youngsters. Of the parents interviewed in Vancouver, 46% agreed with the young peoples' opti-mism. The British Asians, on the other hand, expressed grave doubts about obtaining equality of opportunity with their white peers (Table 2.32) and they were realistic about the prevalent racial discrimination and ways to cope with it. The intention to stay on for further education and/or to go for higher education or, if everything failed, to work in their family business, are some of the ways in which they hoped to overcome this disadvantage. The parents in Birmingham affirmed this situation.

However, the British Asian young people and the parents were of the opin-ion that there is no racism in schools. But the majority of Asian and white teach-ers from Birmingham commented upon the degree of racism embedded in school structures. Most thought it covert, but it is expressed openly through derogatory remarks about the Asians and the blacks.

The following are some examples: a senior teacher calling Urdu 'Da da' language, 'It is up to the parents to change not the school', 'If they want to practice their religion and customs why don't they go home? They are lucky to be here; they would be starving in Bangledesh', 'If we are so bad why are they so desperate to come here — under the heavy lorries, in fridges.' Some teachers also like listening to and telling racist jokes. It may be argued that such 'light-hearted' comments are innocuous as long as teachers are fair in the classroom. But such remarks may be an expression of a deeper level of social prejudice and should be a cause for concern (also see DES, 1985).

Joly (1987) interviewed 35 Kashmiri families in Birmingham and found that only 8 families (22%) referred to an incident of a racial nature. But the author comments: 'We have good reasons to assume that these incidents happen more often than parents realise. The children keep it to themselves and do not care to make a fuss of it at home' (p. 25). In a large-scale study in 20 urban comprehensive schools, Smith & Tomlinson (1989) found that only 1% of parents reported racial incidents and only eight out of 2,074 parents mentioned racial prejudice among teachers. Troyna & Hatcher (1992), in their book, challenge these findings and goes on to show that a high degree of racism is to be found in primary schools. Gibson (1988) carried out an in-depth study of Punjab's Jat Sikh community and their school-age youngsters in California. She found that the parents and students did not think there was any prejudice amongst teachers. The parents thought that teachers are good and capable people. But informal interviews with high-school teachers revealed a strong and unmistakable undercurrent of prejudice (p. 178).

Taylor & Hegarty (1985), in a comprehensive review of studies on British Asian students, report: 'there may be fairly fine dividing lines between preferences, prejudices and racism, especially when an attempt is made to assess both overt and covert manifestations. The evidence that does exist suggests a much lower incidence of prejudice among teachers than the general population and that 10% of teachers may be prejudiced to some degree. The few studies of Asian parents suggest that they do not see teachers as prejudiced but are only too aware of the dedication and concern which they invest in the work.

It seems to me that, though parents commend most teachers' professionalism there is a significant number of teachers who believe in assimilation and are intolerant of the Asian way of life. Gibson (1986: 197) reports that most teachers in the high school believed in assimilation and some were even racists.

From the interview data, it became clear that the young people in both cities were developing bicultural identities. This was being achieved through the twin processes of sharp differentiation in some areas of behaviour and synthesis in others. The process of differentiation implies a clear demarcation of boundaries between home and school norms in certain domains. For instance, direct questioning of an elder's opinion is considered very rude in most Asian families (perhaps in some British families too), but schools at least purport to encourage questioning and probing attitudes. Most Asian young people learn to separate these 'situations' in their minds and behave accordingly. I have met Sikh girls who are bright and extroverted at schools, but who take a more passive role at home to keep the peace in the family. The synthesis of cultural traditions is taking place in food, dress, music (Asian videos/English TV), mixed friendship, humour and bilingualism. There is a lot of evidence (in Chapter 2) to support the thesis that young people are becoming familiar with both their home culture and that of the host society.

However, 'synthesising' of two cultures can also lead to creative tension and compartmentalising of experiences. Meera Syal, a writer of Indian origin, described her experiences to the Guardian reporter (14th May, 1991):

> Syal describes her life as schizophrenic, acknowledging that much of the creative impetus for her writing and performing comes from the clash of two cultures she has grown up with ... a lot of women of my generation see the qualities in both cultures and find them perplexing, but a amusing not desperate ... My feelings on the whole is compassionate. Maybe I should be angrier. '

Shaikh & Kelly (1989) interviewed 50 Muslim girls in Manchester on a range of cultural and social issues. Their conclusion reads as follows.

> The picture that emerges from this research as that from Miles (1984), is of British girls from Pakistan families who are successfully mixing the two traditions and creating their own way of living ... the task is to mix and match cultures to create their own design (p. 18).

Drury (1991) worked with Sikh girls in Nottingham and came to a similar conclusion:

> I found that my respondents were neither fully culturally assimilated into white British culture, nor entirely encapsulated within their parental culture ... my study on the whole indicted that my respondents were relatively conversant and comfortable with both socio-cultures and, consequently, were sometimes able to exhibit a contextual culture based on selective and situational decisions (p. 388).

Gibson (1988) found that the Jat Punjabi Sikh youngsters, who were brought up in America, became quite proficient in the ways of the dominant culture. She draws the following conclusion from her research:

> Parents firmly instruct their young to add what is good from majority ways to their own but not to lose what is significant about their Punjabi heritage. Young people, for their part, adopt more of the majority group's values than their parents would like, but still resist assimilation and, like

other parents, resent the pressures on them to change (p. 198).

The majority of our respondents — young people, parents, community leaders and teachers — thought that schools ought to make provision for the teaching of community languages within the curriculum. The issue of teaching community languages is a controversial one. On the one hand, there are educationalists (Cummins, 1988; Skutnabb-Kangas, 1988; Tosi, 1988; Bourne 1989) who are convinced of the educational, cultural and social benefits of enlightened bilingual/multilingual policies for all schools. On the other hand, there are some parents, teachers and liberal academics who, on pragmatic grounds, favour ethnic communities being responsible for the teaching of their own languages and culture. Cummins (1988) argues that it is imperative that minority students' languages and cultures are included in the school curriculum and that teaching methods promote an interactionist stance in which students actively participate with their linguistic and cultural experiences. Such a policy would be based on the notion that bilingualism is an additive experience. Cummins writes:

> Although policy with respect to linguistic (as compared with cultural) incorporation has tended to be vague and ambivalent, the linguistic component is regarded central to the present framework on the grounds that a multicultural policy which ignores linguistic diversity is vacuous and there is considerable research evidence showing the importance of linguistic component for minority students' academic achievement (pp. 138–9).

Skutnabb-Kangas (1988: 33) asserts that democratic countries should promote bilingualism as a matter of right for its minority communities so that students can fully participate in civic society. He believes in the 'enrichment theories' and argues that the child's mother-tongue and cultural social background should be a positive starting point for the school. The existence of minorities is seen as costly but enriching for societies, and bilingualism/biculturalism is seen as beneficial and stimulating for the child.

Tosi (1988: 96) sketches the half-hearted and fragmentary effort of the DES (now DSE) on community languages in British schools and concludes by stating that multicultural policies should include strong commitment to bilingualism. Bourne (1989) carried out a comprehensive study of 'Education Provision for Bilingual Pupils' in England and Wales. Her report is wide-ranging and rich in details on policy and the provision of English language teaching, English language support, community languages and bilingual support. However, her main conclusion is that ethnic languages are here to stay and it is important that the policy-makers (DES and LEAs) should formulate coherent policies on bilingualism/multilingualism. She urges practitioners and others to learn from the Welsh experience and to promote a bilingual perspective in schools, which should enhance the cognitive development and cultural enrich-ment of all pupils. She argues:

> In a number of schools the percentages of pupils sharing the same lan-guages are such that the development of full bilingual education pro-grammes would seem to be perfectly feasible, if desired by the local community ... for example, in one town visited, out of four secondary schools, three were almost all white, while a third had over 70% of black and bilingual pupils (p. 198).

Steiner-Khamsi (1990) argues that the recent 1988 Education Reform Act leaves the issues of community languages (in England and Wales) untouched; if anything it further marginalises them and leaves them to the idiosyncratic poli-cies of LEAs and schools. Mackinon & Densham (1989), in a cogently argued paper, came to the conclusion that the present central policies on community languages in England would lead to a homogenised state rather than a multicul-tural one.

On the opposite side of this debate are some Asian parents, teachers and academics (e.g. Gibson, 1988; Stones, 1980) who believe that schools ought to concentrate on enabling ethnic students to gain good academic and voca-tional qualifications so that they can compete with their white peers to some advantage. Also, it is felt that the available resources should be used to teach English so that they can become fully conversant with the language. Rex (1965) writes:

> The teaching of mother tongue is of separate importance. What minority people want is to have financial support so that it can be used to enlarge the cultural experiences of the group. It cannot in the kind of society which we have in mind here ever attain anything like equality with the main language in some sort of bilingual state. But there is no reason why minority people should not be able to express themselves and communicate with each other about their experiences in their own language (p. 12).

The ethnic communities from the Indian sub-continent are deeply divided along the lines or religious, caste and regional affiliations. There is no strong movement by ethnic parents to advance the cause of community language teach-ing in Birmingham or Vancouver. For instance, Punjabi-speaking Hindus and Muslims want their children to learn Hindi and Urdu respectively and not Punjabi as this is deemed to be the language of the Sikhs. In reviewing, briefly, the bilingual situation in Wales, Bourne comments (1989: 194) 'it requires an act of will for minority communities to retain and pass on their languages and cultures, and this commitment must be a crucial factor in encouraging young people to choose teaching as a profession'.

The Muslim community in the UK is very well organised. It has centres for Islamic studies in large cities; London, Manchester and Leeds centres are very active in offering courses for teachers and others. There is also a Muslim forum for articulating the needs and demands of Muslim communities. The Observer reported (2nd August 1992: 2):

> There are more than 21 full-time private Muslim schools in Britain and these schools will apply to opt-in to the state sector. This has been accomplished through a well-organised campaign by the Muslim Education Co-ordinating Committee UK.

However, the other Asian communities in the UK are less organised and are not likely to press their demands in a well-organised and cohesive way. The Sikh community in Vancouver runs a private secondary school and is reasonably well organised. The Sikhs are also planning to open primary schools in Abbotsfield, Surrey and Mission — in British Columbia.

In my judgement, the lack of qualified second-generation bilingual teachers is going to be the major difficulty in implementing even the most modest programme of community language teaching in Britain and Canada. Ideally, of course, if it is planned to preserve the community/heritage languages, we need bilingual schools as in Wales (Baker, 1985). But in my view this will remain a distant goal in Britain, given the present government's lack of policies on multicultural and bilingual education. Therefore, it seems to me that schools with a significant ethnic intake could offer up to two or three community languages within the school curriculum, with properly qualified staff and adequate resources (including books and other materials). The Birmingham schools included in the present survey offer at least one ethnic language. Likewise, the study schools in Vancouver offer Mandarin as one of the community languages. More financial help could be provided to the ethnic communities to improve the educational facilities of the supplementary and weekend schools. In my experience, the communities' current efforts to teach their languages are not very effective. This is borne out by the present research. Only a small number of students were fully literate in their mother-tongue, though the Muslim youngsters were better than the Hindus or Sikhs. Community schools are often in cramped old buildings and usually staffed by part-timers who are not fully qualified (Ghuman & Wong, 1989). The material used is mostly imported from the countries of origin, though attempts are being made to produce material in Britain and Canada. Attendances at such schools are intermittent. Due to large classes, teachers use rote-learning methods, thereby demotivating students who are more used to 'activity methods' of learning. If the schools are to become more effective and attractive to ethnic students, they would need substantial financial help, advice and support from local authorities.

From the interview and acculturation scale data, interesting differences between the Muslim boys and girls and others were highlighted. The Muslim young people are more religious-minded in that they attend Mosques regularly, and know more about their religion in contrast to their Hindu and Sikh peers (Table 2.21). This inference is also supported by the interview data from parents. The Muslim parents (though small in number) tended to be more concerned about the religious education of children and young people. Their concern was particularly marked in relation to the education of girls. They would prefer single-sex schools, whereas the Hindu and Sikh parents feel that the way to achieve inter-cultural understanding is to follow the norms of the host society. The Muslim parents are also in favour of establishing voluntary-aided secondary schools where the education of young people can be run along Islamic principles. Their efforts to achieve this goal is nearer to fruition as the community has been given the green light by Mr Patten, the present Secretary of State of Education in England and Wales (The Observer, 14th August 1992).

The Hindu and Sikh young people interviewed in Birmingham and Vancouver were woefully ignorant of their respective religions (Chapter 2:53). The main reason for this is the lack of properly organised religious instruction in the temple and Gurudwaras: ceremonies and services follow the same pattern as that originally established centuries ago in India, which the young people do not understand. Parents, though willing to teach religion within the family circle, do not have the time to do so. If the Hindu and Sikh communities want their younger generation to follow in their footsteps, they have to seriously re-think their strategies in order to teach religion in a more structured and organised way. A Hindu community leader from Birmingham sounded a warning:

> Parents do not have the background and knowledge to explain to their children the basics of their religions. For instance, parents say: Hanuman (one of the Hindu Gods) had a tail. Kids say why? They have no answer to such questions ... next generation would carry only 25–30% of our religious knowledge and influence, then it will go down. Mandirs (Hindu Temples) and Gurudwaras will be empty — owls would howl in these places (translated from Hindi), Brahamins and Bhais (Sikh priest) can't speak English — tell me how can young people learn? Muslims are full of zeal, they are doing better! Mosques are full.

The majority of parents interviewed in this study are coming around to accepting their young people's biculturalism. They approve of bilingualism, change of food habits, and modified school uniform (in the UK) and respect their choice of friends. However, parents are more cautious in giving girls the same degree of freedom and choice as boys, particularly Muslim parents. Parental fears are founded on the alarming and horrific stories they hear and read of wanton drunkenness, promiscuous sex (with the added danger of AIDS), drug abuse and football hooliganism. For instance, when I was carrying out the present research in summer 1990, the Vancouver School Board decided to go ahead with the installation of condom machines in high schools despite strong opposition from the Indo-Canadian community.

I heard informally from several teachers that parents are beginning to turn a blind eye to (or even accept) dating. Some are accepting love marriages 'perforce'; others are modifying their rigid customs and allowing limited courtships. But there are some parents who are very orthodox and would not allow any deviance from established norms and practice. But, overall, the picture which emerges from my inquiry is encouraging and optimistic. Most parents and young people are learning to make compromises on a whole range of social and educational matters (Chapter 4:121). Several other researchers found a similar trend (Bhachu, 1985b). She described the life-styles of the Sikhs from the East Africa as changing from kinship-orientated to couple-orientated, and adds:

> Thus marriage is not seen so much as an alliance between families as a union between two people: an adoption of the indigenous British society's focus on the individual. This feature, combined with others such as the increased earning powers and independence of the women, the predominance of nuclear household which tend to loosen kinship obligations, and modifications of traditional criteria of spouse selection, are all indicative of developing individualism (p. 164).

She also argues that the young Asians are synthesising British cultural values with traditional values and are developing new cultural patterns. In this context, it is relevant to quote the main conclusion of Stopes-Roe & Cochran's (1990) research with young people in Birmingham:

> The majority felt they belonged in Britain, that it was their home, and they wanted their children to live here in Britain, so they can be citizens of this country. For the most part they believed in their future. It seemed their biggest task would not be, as many think that it is, to persuade their parents to believe in and to cooperate with this future, but to convince the natives of its possibilities and benefits (p. 209).

Teachers, counsellors and social workers are also major players in this drama of life. If they choose to be antipathetic to Asian cultural values and traditions and feel that the Western way of life is superior to the Asian, then it is likely that their attitudes will lead to conflict, separatism and alienation among their students. On the other hand, if they develop a truly 'sympathetic attitude' and generally cultivate a positive outlook towards ethnic cultures, then there is a strong possibility that the education system will produce balanced, aware and mentally healthy bicultural youngsters.

In this context, it is important to draw the attention of the reader to the generous provision of student counsellors in Vancouver high schools — four in each school I researched. They play a very important part, along with home-school link workers, in helping ethnic students to resolve some of their conflicts, anxieties and worries. In Britain, form tutors are supposed to perform this task. Regrettably, due to the pressure of work and lack of training, individual counselling is very much a hit-and-miss affair. Other researchers have also drawn attention to this problem (Purewal, 1976; Walker, 1981).

The academic achievement and general progress of British-Asian and Indo-Canadian students is rated as average to above average by teachers. Some teachers in our sample argued that a number of young people may not be realising their full potential due to their handicap in English, particularly written English. Two Asian teachers from Birmingham suggested that the low achievement of some students may be due to the low expectations of white teachers. An Asian headmistress argued that below average performance in inner-city schools, where the majority of Asian and black students are concentrated, may be due to poor teaching and inadequate resources. These sentiments find a resonance in the responses of white teachers to Ranger (1988: 58):

Many of the white teachers also mentioned the low expectations they felt some of their colleagues had of ethnic minority pupils, an attitude which was sometimes reflected in some white teacher's perceptions of their ethnic minority colleagues. Other sources of discrimination mentioned by white teachers were: Euro-centered curricula and lack of awareness among some white teachers of ethnic minority cultures.

The actual evidence on the performance of British Asian students has been equivocal. Part of the difficulty lies in using the generic 'South Asians/Asians': this includes such diverse groups as upper caste and professional Hindus, middle-class/caste Jat Sikhs, Mirpuri and Bangladeshi Muslims from rural backgrounds, and Westernised Hindus, Sikhs and Muslims from East Africa. But a recent large-scale study by Smith & Tomlinson (1989) draws the following conclusions on the achievement of British Asian students:

The exam results over all subjects are slightly poorer among pupils originating from the Indian sub-continent and from the West Indies than among those of UK origin' (p. 250);

and further on

Among young people leaving school, differences in educational attainment between the racial minorities and whites are not very large. With the exception of some specific groups, Asians are now obtaining similar results to whites (p. 304).

The specific groups they refer to are students of Muslim parents from Bangladesh and Pakistan (also see recent report of the Policy Studies Institute; Jones, 1993). It is imperative to note that the diverse ethnic groups from the Indian sub-continent have unique histories, aspirations, motivations and cultural resources to help them to realise the educational potential of their children and young people. For instance, Gibson (1988) found that Punjabi Sikh students in California performed better than their white peers despite their difficulties with English and the fact that they suffered from 'racism' in the high school they attended. The major reasons for this success are the hard work which the students put in and the high aspirations that Punjabi parents have for their children.

The parents in the present study were satisfied with their young people's education; Indo-Canadians more so than the Asians in Birmingham (Tables 4.3 and 4.4). The Birmingham parents in the study expressed their concern over inadequate homework and dissatisfaction with school discipline. A similar reservation was expressed by Punjabi and Bengali/Bangladeshi parents in my previous research (Ghuman, 1980, Ghuman & Gallop, 1981). However, Smith & Tomlinson (1989: 61) found that Asian parents were slightly more satisfied with their youngsters' education than white parents, but Bangladeshi parents were less so.

As regards parents' active involvement (e.g. helping with homework and frequent visits to schools), the parents in the study are not that actively involved. Reasons for such a lack of participation were given in Chapter 4:110.

An interesting view is taken by Bhachu (1985b: 9) on this issue. She suggests that Sikh parents in England fall into two main categories: interventionist and non-interventionist. Interventionists are those parents who are actively involved in helping their children to achieve educational qualifications. These parents have direct access to, and knowledge of, the educational system. They utilise the system in various ways to advance their children's education; for example, private schooling and paid tuition. Non-interventionists, however, are generally less educated than parents from more urban interventionist backgrounds. But their motivation and aspirations for their children are just as high, although they are less actively involved. Their children are as likely to achieve academic success as those of the interventionists, according to Bhachu. Gibson (1988) warns us of the danger of the 'so-called middle class notion of involvement' being the universal model for all parents, thereby disadvantaging ethnic minorities and working-class students by running a teaching system which requires the active engagement of parents (e.g. in project work and field trips).

From the evidence presented in Chapter 5 it is discouraging to note that the ethnic communities in both cities are ineffective in providing recreational and sports facilities for their young people. Their main concern is still with the first-generation, providing for their religious and social needs. Communities have yet to develop resources to institute new mechanisms and to initiate changes in their places of worship that will accommodate the needs of Asian-origin young people. If they are to become biculturally competent individuals, they will need the sympathetic understanding and support of their parents, teachers, counsellors and community leaders.

My overall impression is that the young people in the study were making determined efforts to achieve a working synthesis of two cultures. They were lively, aware and sensitive young people and it was a privilege to work with them.

# References

ANDERSON, B.A. and FRIDERES, S.J. 1981, *Ethnicity in Canada: Theoretical Perspectives*. Toronto: Butterworths.

ANWAR, M. 1978, *Between Two Cultures*. London: Commission for Racial Equality.

—1979, *The Myth of Return: Pakistanis in Britain*. London:Heineman.

—1985, *Pakistanis in Britain: A Sociological Study*. London: New Century Publishers.

—1988, Muslims, community and the issues in education. In B. O'KEEFE (ed.) *Schools for Tomorrow* Lewes: Falmer Press.

—1991, Race relations policies in Britain: Agenda for the 1990s. *Policy Paper in Ethnic Relations* No. 21. Warwick: Centre for Research in Ethnic Relations.

ASHRAF, A.S. 1988, A view of education — An Islamic perspective. In B. O'KEEFE (ed.) *Schools for Tomorrow* (pp. 69–80). London: The Falmer Press.

AURORA, G.S. 1967, *The New Frontiersmen*. Bombay: Popular Prakasham.

BAGLEY, C. 1982, Achievement, behaviour disorder and social circumstances in West Indian children and other ethnic groups. In K.G. VERMA and C. BAGLEY (eds) *Self-concept Achievement and Multicultural Education*. London: Macmillan.

—1989, Education for all: A Canadian dimension. In K.G. VERMA (ed.) *Education for All: A Landmark in Pluralism* (pp. 98–117). London: The Falmer Press.

BAKER, C. 1985, *Aspects of Bilingualism in Wales*. Clevedon: Multilingual Matters.

BALLARD, R. and BALLARD, C. 1979, The development of South Asian settlements in Britain. In J.L. WATSON (ed.) *Between Two Cultures*. Oxford: Basil Blackwell.

BATH, K.S. 1972, The distribution and spatial patterns of Punjabi population in Wolverhampton. Unpublished MA thesis, Aberystwyth: University of Wales.

BERLIN, I. 1989, *The Crooked Timber of Humanity*. London: John Murray.

BERRY, J.W., KIM, V., POWERS, S., YOUNG, M. and BUJAKI, 1989, Acculturation attitudes in plural societies. *Applied Psychology, An International Review* 38(2), 185–206.

BHACHU, P. 1985a, *Twice Migrants: East African Sikh Settlers in Britain*. London: Tavistock.

—1985b, Parental education strategies: The case of Punjabi Sikhs in Britain. *Research Papers in Ethnic Relations* No. 3. Warwick: Centre for Research in Ethnic Relations.

—1985c, Multilingual education: Parental views. *New Community* 12, 1, 9–21.

BHATNAGAR, J. 1981, Multiculturalism and education of immigrants in Canada. In J. BHATNAGAR (ed.) *Educating Immigrants*. London: Croom Helm.

BOURNE, J. 1989, *Moving into the Mainstream. LEA Provision for Bilingual Pupils*. Windsor: NFER-Nelson.

BROWN, C. 1984, *Black and White Britain: The Third PSI Survey*. London: Gower.

BUCHIGNANI, N., INDRA, M.D. and SCRIVASTIVA, R. 1985, *Continuous Journey: A Social History of South Asians in Canada*. Toronto: McMelland Stewart Ltd in association with Multiculturalism Directorate.

CHADNEY, G.J. 1980, Sikh family patterns and ethnic adaptation in Vancouver. *Ambrasia* 7, 1, 121–30.

CUMMINS, J. 1988, From multicultural to anti-racist education: An analysis of programmes and policies in Ontario. In T. SKUTTNABB-KANGAS and J. CUMMINS (eds) *Minority Education* (pp 127–160). Cleveland: Multilingual Matters.

DAHYA, B. 1972, Pakistanis in England. *New Community* 2, 25–33.

DAVEY, A. *et al.*, 1983, *Learning to be Prejudiced: Growing up in Multi-ethnic Britain.* London: Edward Arnold.

DESAI, R. 1963, *Indian Immigrants in Britain.* London: Oxford University Press.

Department of Education and Science (DES) 1985, *Education for All* (The Swann Report). London: HMSO.

DHAMI, S.S. 1988, *Maluka.* Amritsar: Balraj Sahni Press.

DREVER, J. 1962, *A Dictionary of Psychology.* Harmondsworth: Penguin Books.

DRURY, B. 1991, Sikh girls and the maintenance of an ethnic culture. *New Community* 17(3), 387–400.

ERICKSON, H.E. 1968, *Identity: Youth and Crisis.* London: Faber & Faber.

FISHER, D. and ECHOLS, F. 1989, Evaluation report on the Vancouver School Board's Race Relations Policy. Vancouver: Vancouver School Board.

FRYER, P. 1984, *Staying Power: The History of Black People in Britain.* London: Pluto Press.

GHUMAN, P.A.S. 1975, *The Cultural Context of Thinking: A ComparativeStudy of Punjabi and English Boys.* Slough: National Foundation for Educational Research.

—1980a, Bhattra Sikhs in Cardiff: Family and kinship organisation. *New Community* 8, 3, 308–16.

—1980b, Punjabi parents and English education. *Educational Research* 22, 2, 121–30.

—1991a, Best or worst of two worlds: A study of Asian adolescents. *Educational Research* 33, 2, 121–32.

—1991b, Have they passed the cricket test? A qualitative study of Asian adolescents. *Journal of Multilingual and Multicultural Development* 12, 5, 327–46.

—1992, Asian teachers in British schools: A qualitative study (p. 33). Unpublished research paper, Faculty of Education, University of Wales, Aberystwyth.

GHUMAN, P.A.S. and BLAKE, M. 1987, Education of Bangladeshi children in Sylhet and London. *British Journal of Psychology* 57, 100.

GHUMAN, P.A.S. and GALLOP, R. 1981, Educational attitudes of Bengali families in Cardiff. *Journal of Multilingual and Multicultural Development* 2, 2, 127–44.

GHUMAN, P.A.S. and WONG, R. 1989, Chinese parents and English education. *Educational Research* 31, 2, 134–40.

GIBSON, M.A. 1988, *Accommodation without Assimilation.* Ithaca and London: Cornell University Press.

GREEN, J. 1990, *Them: Voices from the Immigrant Community in Contemporary Britain.* London: Secker & Warburg.

ISLAMIA, 1992, *National Muslim Newsletter* No. 19. Islamia Publishers, Schools Trust.

JOLY, D. 1987, Making a place for Islam in British society: Muslims in Birmingham. *Research Papers in Ethnic Relations* No. 4. Warwick: Centre for Research in Ethnic Relations.

JONES, T. 1993, *Britain's Ethnic Minorities: An Analysis of the Labour Force Survey.* London: Policy Studies Institute.

KERLINGER, N. 1970, *Foundations of Behavioural Research.* London: Holt, Rinehart and Winston.

KHAN, S.V. 1979, The Pakistanis: Mirpuri villagers at home and in Bradford. In J.L. WATSON (ed.) *Between Two Cultures.* Oxford: Basil Blackwell.

KITWOOD, T. 1983, Self-conception among young British-Asian Muslims: Confrontation of a sterotype. In G. BLACKWELL (ed.) *Threatened Identities*. Chichester: Wiley.

KLUCKHOLN, F.R. and STRODBECK, F.L. 1961, *Variations in Value Orientations*. Chicago: Row, Peterson.

KNIGHT, G.G. 1988, The expectations and priorities of Muslim parents, residing in the Small Heath area of Birmingham, regarding their children's education. Unpublished OTTO Fellowship Dissertation Spring Term, Faculty of Education University of Birmingham.

KONADOPI, C. 1949, *Indian Overseas, 1838–1949*. New Delhi: Indian Council of World Affairs.

KROGER, J. 1989, *Identity in Adolescence*. London: Routledge.

LIKERT, R. 1932, A technique for the measurement of attitudes. *Archive Psychology* No. 140.

MACKINON, K and DENSHAM, J. 1989, Ethnolinguistic diversity in Britain: Policies and practices in school and society. *Language, Culture and Curriculum* 2,2,75–89.

MACLURE, S. 1988, *Education Reformed*. Sevenoaks: Hodder & Stoughton.

MILES, S. 1984, Asian girls and the transition from school to ...? In S. BALL (ed.) *Comprehensive Schooling: A Reader*. Lewes: Falmer Press.

NORTHOVER, M. 1989, Ethnic identity in Gujarati/English bilingual language and social context. Paper presented at the Second Regional Conference of IACCP Amsterdam, The Netherlands, 27th July–1st August 1989.

NAIPAUL, V.S. 1991, *India: A Million Mutinies Now*. London: Minerva.

OSLER, A. 1989, *Speaking Out: Black Girls in Britain*. London: Virago Upstarts.

PAREKH, B. 1986, The structure of authority within the Indian family. In K.A. BRAH (ed.) *Working with Asian Young People*. London: National Association for Asian Youth.

PETERSON, C. 1988, *Personality*. London & San Diego: Harcourt Brace.

PHINNEY, S.J. and ROTHERAM, J.M. (eds) 1987, *Children's Ethnic Socialization: Pluralism and Development*. London: Sage.

PUREWAL, A. 1976, Home/school relationships of Punjabis in Bedford. Unpublished MSc thesis, Cranfield Institute of Technology.

RANGER, C. 1988, *Ethnic Minority School Teachers*. London: Commission for Racial Equality.

REX, J. 1965, The concept of a multicultural society. *Occasional Papers in Ethnic Relations* 3. Warwick: Centre for Research in Ethnic Relations.

REX, J. and TOMLINSON, S. 1979, *Colonial Immigrants in a British City: A Class Analysis*. London: Routledge and Kegan Paul.

ROSE, E.J.B. *et al.* 1969, *Colour and Citizenship: A Report on British Race Relations*. London: Oxford University Press.

ROSENTHAL, A.D. 1987, Ethnic identity development in adolescents. In S.J. PHINNEY and J.M. ROTHERM (eds) *Children's Ethnic Socialization: Pluralism and Development*. London: Sage Publications.

SHARAN-JEET, Shan 1986, *An Autobiography*. London: The Women's Press.

SHARMA, V. 1971, *Rampal and His Family*. London: Collins.

SHAIKH, S. and KELLY, A. 1989, To mix or not to mix: Pakistani girls in British schools. *Educational Research* 31, 1, 10–19.

SHAW, A. 1988, *A Pakistani Community in Britain*. London: Basil Blackwell.

SCHOOLS COUNCIL 1981, Multi-ethnic education: The way forward. Schools Council Pamphlet 18. London: Schools Council.

SINGH, S. 1966, *Philosophy of Sikhism*. Ludhiana: Chardi Kala.

SKUTNABB-KANGAS, T. 1988, Multilingualism and the education of minority children. In T. SKUTNABB-KANGAS and J. CUMMINS (eds) *Minority Education* (pp. 9–44).

Clevedon: Multilingual Matters.

SKUTNABB-KANGAS, T. and CUMMINS, J. (eds) 1988, *Minority Education.* Clevedon: Multilingual Matters.

SMITH, D. J. and TOMLINSON, S. 1989, *The School Effect. A Study of Multi-racial Comprehensives.* London: Policy Studies Institute.

STEINER-KHAMSI, G. 1990, Community languages and anti-racist education: The open battle-field. *Educational Studies* 16, 1, 33–47.

STONES, M. 1980, *The Education of the Black Child in Britain: The Myth of Multiracial Education.* London: Fontana.

STOPES-ROE, M. and COCHRANE, R. 1990, *Citizens of this Country: The Asian-British.* Clevedon: Multilingual Matters.

TAYLOR, J.H. 1976, *The Half-way Generation.* Windsor: NFER.

TAYLOR, M.J. and HEGARTY, S. 1985, *The Best of Both Worlds ....?.* Windsor: NFER-NELSON.

THOMPSON, M. 1974, The second generation — Punjabi or English? *New Community* 3, 3, 242–8.

TOMLINSON, S. 1984, *Home and School in Multicultural Britain.* London: Batsford Academic.

— 1991, Education and training. *New Community* 18, 11, 133–40.

TOSI, A. 1988, The jewel in the crown of the modern prince: The new approach to bilingualism in multicultural education in England. In T. SKUTTNABB-KANGAS and J. CUMMINS (eds) *Minority Education* (pp 79–102). Clevedon: Multilingual Matters.

TRIANDIS, C.H. 1991, Individualism and collectivism. Invited address to the IACCP Conference, Debreccen, Hungary 4–7 July, 1991, 7–33.

TROYNA, B. 1990, Reform or deform? The 1988 Education Reform Act and racial equality in Britain. *New Community* 16, 3, 403–17.

TROYNA, B. and HATCHER, R. 1992, *Racism in Children's Lives.* London: Routledge.

VAIDYANATHAN, P. and NAIDOO, J. 1991, Asian Indians in western countries: Cultural identity and the arranged marriage. In N. BLEICHRODT and P.J.D. DRENTH (eds) *Contemporary Issues in Cross-cultural Psychology.* Amsterdam: Swets & Leitlinger.

VANCOUVER SCHOOLS BOARD, 1989, Guidelines for implementation of VSB race relations policy. Vancouver: Vancouver School Board.

VERMA, K. G. 1986, *Ethnicity and Educational Achievement in British Schools.* London: Macmillan.

— (ed.), 1989, *Education For All: A Landmark in Pluralism.* London: The Falmer Press.

VERNON, P. E. 1969, *Intelligence and Cultural Environment.* London: Methuen.

VERKUTEN, M. 1989, Self-concept in cross-cultural perpectives: Turkishand Dutch adolescents in the Netherlands. Paper read at the 2nd Regional IACC Conference, Amsterdam.

WADE, B and SOUTER, P. 1991, *Continuing to Think: The British Asian Girl.* Clevedon: Multilingual Matters.

WAKIL, P.S., SIDDIQUE, C.M. and WAKIL, A.F. 1981, Between two cultures: A study in socialization of children of immigrants. *Journal of Marriage and the Family* 43, 929–40.

WALKER, A. 1981, Asian girls shelter from fear. *New Society* 58, 994, 418–19.

WATSON, L.J. (ed.) 1979, *Between Two Cultures: Migrants and Minorities in Britain.* Oxford: Basil Blackwell.

WEINREICH, P. 1983, Emerging from threatened identities. In G.M. BREAKWELL (ed.)

*Threatened Identities*. Chichester: John Wiley.

WHORF, B.L. 1956, *Language, Thought and Reality*. Cambridge, MA: MIT Press.

WITKIN, H.A. and BERRY, J.M. 1975, Psychological differentiation in cross-cultural perspective. *Journal of Cross-Cultural Psychology* 6, 4–87.

WILSON, A. 1978, *Finding a Voice: Asian Women in Britain*. London: Virago.

WISEMAN, S. 1966, *Education and Environment*. Manchester: Manchester University Press.

# Appendices

## Appendix 1. Acculturation Scale Used with Birmingham Sample (* = reverse scoring)

1    Girls and boys should be treated the same .............................SA A U D SD

2.    We should celebrate Christmas as we celebrate our own religious festivals .....................................................................SA A U D SD

3.*    Our own customs and traditions are best for us ......................SA A U D SD

4.    I have no wish to go back to the country that my parents came from ...............................................................................SA A U D SD

5.    I would like to see boys and girls from our community going out with English boys and girls.....................................SA A U D SD

6.*    I would rather eat our own food all the time...........................SA A U D SD

7.*    We should always try to fulfil our parents' wishes.................SA A U D SD

8.    We should stay for school dinners ............................................SA A U D SD

9.*    We are better off living with people from our own countries ..................................................................................SA A U D SD

10.    Parents and children should live on their own and not with grandparents and uncles.............................................SA A U D SD

11.*    A woman's place is in the home ...............................................SA A U D SD

12.*    Only our own doctors can understand our illnesses................SA A U D SD

13.*    I would only like to make friends with my own countrymen................................................................................SA A U D SD

14.*    We should learn to speak and write our own language...........SA A U D SD

15.    Sometimes we should cook English food in our homes .........SA A U D SD

16.    We should alter our names so that our teachers can say them easily .............................................................................SA A U D SD

17.    It is good for us to learn something about Christianity...........SA A U D SD

18.    We (boys and girls) should be allowed to meet each other in youth clubs.................................................................SA A U D SD

19.*    I would prefer to live in an area where there are families from our own community .......................................................SA A U D SD

20.    We should visit the homes of our English friends ..................SA A U D SD

21.*    Our films are more entertaining than English films................SA A U D SD

22.    We should ignore our own language if we want to get on in this country.................................................................SA A U D SD

23.* I feel very uneasy with the English ............................SA A U D SD
24.  There should be more marriages between our people
     and the English ................................................................SA A U D SD
25.* Marriages should be arranged by the family...........................SA A U D SD
26.* I would not like our women to behave like
     English women......................................................................SA A U D SD
27.  We should be allowed to choose our own clothes .................SA A U D SD
28.  We should visit English cinemas and play houses..................SA A U D SD
29.* Men should make all the decisions about the affairs
     of the family .......................................................................SA A U D SD
30.  Our women should wear English clothes................................SA A U D SD

# Appendix 2. Acculturation Scale Used with Vancouver Sample

1.   Girls and boys should be treated the same............................SA A U D SD
2.*  Schools should accept our traditional clothes ........................SA A U D SD
3.*  We should attend our places of worship
     (e.g. Gurudwara, temple) ......................................................SA A U D SD
4.   I have no wish to go back to live in the country my
     parents came from................................................................SA A U D SD
5.   I would like to see boys and girls from our community
     going out with white Canadian boys and girls.......................SA A U D SD
6.*  I would rather eat our own food all the time...........................SA A U D SD
7.*  We should always try to fulfil our parents' wishes.................SA A U D SD
8.   We should celebrate Christmas as we celebrate our own
     religious festivals ................................................................SA A U D SD
9.*  We are better off living with people from our own
     countries..............................................................................SA A U D SD
10.  Parents and children should live on their
     own and not with grandparents and uncles ............................SA A U D SD
11.* A woman's place is in the home .............................................SA A U D SD
12.* Only our own doctors can understand our illnesses................SA A U D SD
13.  We should learn something about Christianity .......................SA A U D SD
14.* We should learn to speak and write our own language...........SA A U D SD
15.  Sometimes we should cook Canadian food in our
     own homes ...........................................................................SA A U D SD
16.  We should alter our names so that our teachers can
     say them easily .....................................................................SA A U D SD
17.* I would only like to make friends with my countrymen .........SA A U D SD
18.  Boys and girls should be allowed to meet each
     other in youth clubs..............................................................SA A U D SD

19.* I would prefer to live in an area where there are
     families from our own community............................................SA A U D SD
20.  We should visit the homes of our white
     Canadian friends ...................................................................SA A U D SD
21.* Our films are more entertaining than English
     language films.........................................................................SA A U D SD
22.  We should ignore our own language if we want to
     get on in this country.............................................................SA A U D SD
23.* I feel very uneasy with white Canadians ...............................SA A U D SD
24.  There should be more marriages between our people
     and white Canadians ..............................................................SA A U D SD
25.* Men should make all the decisions about the affairs
     of the family...........................................................................SA A U D SD
26.* I would not like our women to behave like white
     Canadian women......................................................................SA A U D SD
27.  We should be allowed to choose our own clothes .................SA A U D SD
28.  We should visit English language cinemas
     and playhouses ........................................................................SA A U D SD
29.* Marriages should be arranged by the family...........................SA A U D SD
30.  Our women should wear Canadian
     (European style) clothes..........................................................SA A U D SD

## Appendix 3. Students' Background Questionnaire

PLEASE ANSWER THESE QUESTIONS BY PUTTING A (X) IN THE BOX
FOR THE STATEMENT THAT APPLIES TO YOU.

1.  Boy .................. ( )   or   Girl ................. ( )                     .....
2.  I was born in Canada ............. ( )                                     .....
3.  My age last birthday was 13 ( ), 14 ( ), 15 ( ), 16 ( ) , 18( )        ..
4.  I went to primary school in Canada.    Yes ( ) No ( )              .....
5.  At home we speak only English                        ( )
    At home we speak only our Asian languag             ( )
    At home we speak both English and our Asian language   ( )        .....
6.  What is your father's job?.........................................................................
    .................................................................................................................
7.  What is your mother's job (if she has one) outside the home?...................
    .................................................................................................................
8.  Please state the religion of your family...............................................
9.  Do you take a community newspaper? ..... Yes ( ) ..... No ( )          .....

10. If yes, is this written in:

(a) Your home language? ( ) 1
(b) English only? ( ) 2
(c) Both languages? ( ) 3

Overleaf you will find a number of statements about East Indians living in Canada. We would like to know YOUR OWN views on these topics. Please answer by ringing ONE response for each question.

| | | |
|---|---|---|
| SA | means | STRONGLY AGREE |
| A | means | AGREE |
| U | means | DON'T KNOW |
| D | means | DISAGREE |
| SD | means | STRONGLY DISAGREE |

I would like more Asian language programmes on television        SA A U D SD

## Appendix 4: Students' Interview Schedule

1. Sex          Boy    Girl     2. Father's Job  Non-Manual Manual
                  □      □                          □          □

3. Age   13    14     15     16     4. Mother's Job Non-Manual Manual
          □     □      □      □                         □          □

5. Place of  Canada  India   EA     6. Back to India    Yes       No
   Birth       □       □      □                          □         □

7. Religion   Sikh   Hindu  Moslem  8. Attendance at    Yes       No
                □      □      □         Temple            □         □

9. Language  English  Hindi Bilingual 10. Learning of    Yes       No
                □       □      □          Home Language   □         □

11. Person you admire                12. Own Room        Yes       No
    [                          ]                          □         □

13. Food      Indian Canadian Mixed  14. Members of Family
                □      □      □          [                              ]

15. Family Type      Nuclear Extended 16. Friends Indians Canadian Mixture
                       □      □                     □        □        □

17. Equality of     Yes    No     18. School Leaving    16    Stay on
     Boys & Girls    ☐    ☐                   ☐    ☐

19. Vocational/Professional    Prof.    Voc.    No.Adjustment at school
     Aspiration            ☐     ☐     ☐        ☐

20. Favourite Subject(s)   Human   Science   Maths.   Biology   P.E.
                          ☐      ☐      ☐      ☐     ☐

21. Reading                              22. Asian    Yes    No    Mixed
       [_____]        Music    ☐    ☐    ☐

23. Asian Videos    Yes    No     24. Choice of     Yes    No
                 ☐    ☐        Clothes     ☐    ☐

25. Asian Teachers    Yes    No     26. Equality of     Yes    No
                 ☐    ☐        Opportunity    ☐    ☐

# Appendix 5: Parents' Interview Schedule

1. Age     25    35    45    2. Sex          M    F
            ☐    ☐    ☐               ☐    ☐

3. Family          N    E    4. Job    Non   Manual   Self
                 ☐    ☐         Manual      Employed
                               ☐     ☐     ☐

5. No. of Years   born    5    10    6. Children   P    S    Higher
     in Canada     ☐     ☐    ☐        at School   ☐    ☐

7. Education   B.Matric   Matric   Higher    8. Newspaper     C    E
              ☐      ☐     ☐                  ☐    ☐

9. Home Occupation    Yes    No    10. Religion    H    S    M
                     ☐    ☐             ☐    ☐    ☐

11. Language    E    P    M    12. School    Approve    No
     of Home    ☐    ☐    ☐        Discipline    ☐      ☐

13. Curriculum       Satis.   Not Satis.   14. Home Work    Yes    No
                     ☐     ☐                ☐    ☐

15. Ex. Curricular    Support    No    16. R.E. by School    Yes    No
     Activities     ☐      ☐                  ☐    ☐

17. R.E. at Home          Yes    No    18. Home Language      Yes    No
    & Community           ☐      ☐        by School          ☐      ☐

19. Home Language        Yes    No    20. Food          I      C     Mixed
    by Community          ☐      ☐        at Home       ☐      ☐     ☐

21. Prejudice at         Yes    No    22. Co-           A     Dis.   D.K.
    School                ☐      ☐        education      ☐     ☐      ☐

23. Importance  Some   More   Less   24. Satisfaction  Yes    No    D.K.
    of Family    ☐      ☐      ☐         with School    ☐      ☐      ☐

25. Help with            Yes    No    26. Visited School    Yes    No
    home-work             ☐      ☐                           ☐      ☐

27. School Uniform       Yes    No    28. Equality of       Yes    No
                          ☐      ☐        boys & girls       ☐      ☐

29. Equality in Jobs     Yes    No    30. Voc. Aspirations  High   Low
                          ☐      ☐                           ☐      ☐

31. Choice of Friends    Yes    No    32. Choice of Clothes  Yes    No
                          ☐      ☐                            ☐      ☐

33. Own Room/Radio       Yes    No
                          ☐      ☐

# Appendix 6:  Teachers' Interview Schedule

1. Age   25     35     45     55    2. Ethnicity          White  Others
         ☐      ☐      ☐      ☐                            ☐      ☐

3. Sex                   M      F    4. Prof. Exp.    5     10     15
                         ☐      ☐       in Schools   ☐      ☐      ☐

5. Multicultural Course  Yes    No    6. Exp. of Community  Yes    No
                          ☐      ☐                           ☐      ☐

7. Bilingualism          Yes    No    8. Community          Yes    No
                          ☐      ☐        Languages          ☐      ☐

9. School Uniform        Yes    No   10. Mixed Classes      Yes    No
   (Ethnic dress)         ☐      ☐                           ☐      ☐

11.  Religious Education
     [                    ]

12.  Voc. Aspirations    High    Low
                          [ ]     [ ]

13.  Concerns of Asian Parents
     [                    ]

14.  School leaving       Yes     No
                          [ ]     [ ]

15.  Equality of Sexes    Yes     No
                          [ ]     [ ]

16.  Achievers    High    Av.    Low
                  [ ]     [ ]     [ ]

17.  School Activities    Yes     No
                          [ ]     [ ]

18.  Favourite    Maths  Science  Hum.
     Subjects     [ ]     [ ]      [ ]

19.  Proficiency  Above A    A    Below A
     in English      [ ]    [ ]      [ ]

20.  Friendship   Own    Ethnic   Mixed
                  [ ]     [ ]       [ ]

21.  Parental participation    Yes    No
     & support                 [ ]    [ ]

22.  Adolescents' and their problems:    [                              ]

# Appendix 7:  Technical Features of Acculturation Scales

## Birmingham Sample

(a)    1974 group

    Reliability  Co-efficient (split-half)    =    0.82

    Cronbach $L$    =    0.81

(b)    1987 group

    Reliability  Co-efficient (split-half)    =    0.83

    Cronbach $L$    =    0.78

## Vancouver Sample

    Reliability  Co-efficient (split-half)    =    0.85

    Cronbach $L$    =    0.75

**Note:**  Reliability Co-efficient was calculated by using Spearman-Brown formula.